THE
FIFTH
PHRASE

Also by Dr. Joe Vitale

Faith

Expect Miracles

Zero Limits

The Miracle

The Art and Science of Results

THE FIFTH PHRASE

The Next Ho'oponopono, Zero Limits Healing Stage, and Other Advanced Healing Methods

Dr. Joe Vitale

Published 2021 by Gildan Media LLC
aka G&D Media
www.GandDmedia.com

Front cover design by David Rheinhardt of Pyrographx

Interior design by Meghan Day Healey of Story Horse, LLC

Library of Congress Cataloging-in-Publication Data is available upon request

Paperback ISBN: 978-1-7225-0543-1

10   9   8   7   6   5   4   3   2   1

Contents

Foreword

Joe Vitale may be best known from his appearance in the 2006 movie phenomenon *The Secret*, which explained the law of attraction and how it can help you to be more successful and happy. You may also know Joe from his best-selling book *Zero Limits*, which introduced the world to the secret Hawaiian system of ho'oponopono (pronounced *hoe*-a-pono-pono) and Joe's teacher, Dr. Ihaleakala Hew Len.

Joe Vitale has been changing lives with his original ideas on spiritual growth, the wealth mindset, marketing, and more, for over thirty-five years. Joe wrote his first book, *Zen and the Art of Writing*, way back in 1984. In 2020, G&D Media published his book *The Art and Science of Results*, which features several of his most popular ideas for clearing inner blocks to goals.

Two qualities are particularly relevant to this book. First, Joe has always been on the cutting edge of his topics, whether it is marketing ideas for your business or spiritual growth ideas for your soul. Second, Joe has the unique ability to communicate these ideas in an entertaining, clear, and accessible way that anyone can master and benefit from.

These qualities are particularly relevant to this book. The ideas that follow are truly cutting-edge spiritual teachings. Joe changed the conversation about how to grow personally and spiritually when he revealed the four phrases of ho'oponopono, and how they are so different from traditional ideas based on intention or empowerment.

In this book, Joe reveals his long-awaited fifth phrase, which he had previously only revealed to his advanced ho'oponopono certification clients, and which adds a whole new dimension to this ancient Hawaiian system. He'll also take his original ho'oponopono material to a new, advanced level and teach you how to progress to the next level of spiritual growth, which he calls *awakening*.

This book represents the most cutting-edge content Joe has ever discussed. As you'll soon learn, Joe is not going to communicate these advanced ideas like some inaccessible spiritual guru. He'll address these ideas like a fellow traveler who is walking the spiritual journey alongside you.

In the late 1970s, Joe was homeless in Dallas, struggling in his career, and at an emotional low point. Although he has achieved international acclaim and financial wealth and has grown further emotionally and spiritually than he ever thought possible, he still treats himself as a beginner on the path, and still has the daily personal and spiritual challenges of you, his fellow travelers.

Nevertheless, Joe's lifetime of study, practice, and experience has given him a set of answers for addressing those challenges, and even more importantly, using them as another path of personal growth and discovery. Get ready to go to a whole new level of spiritual understanding as Joe reveals the fifth phrase.

1
Divided No More

This book is about going past our egos, going past the illusions of life, and tapping into what I call *Divinity*. In order for me to be a clear channel of that, I want to begin with a prayer and invocation.

O infinite divine mind, through my beloved high self, cleanse this unit of all negativity, both within and without, that it may be a perfect vessel for your presence.

Right now in our society, there seems to be numerous divisions around cultural questions, politics, income, and many other things. At the same time, we hear that individually people are experiencing higher levels of anxiety, depression, and other emotional issues than, say, twenty years prior.

Let's begin with a quote used by my teacher, Dr. Hew Len, although it goes back further, to an 1858 speech given by Abraham Lincoln and ultimately to the Bible (Matthew 12:25; Luke 11:17): "A house divided against itself cannot stand." This is true for nations, communities, organizations, and families as well as individuals. In the house of humanity, the individual is the common denominator. When the individual is divided, the house is divided.

Today the divisions seem more intense and rampant than twenty years ago, but I believe that's a narrow view of the situation. Because I've written books on P. T. Barnum, cofounder of Barnum & Bailey Circus, from the 1800s, and on inspirational author Bruce Barton from the 1920s, I have a sense of what people were going through at different time periods. Most recently, I've been investigating the ancient Greek philosophical school of Stoicism, so I have an interest in what was going on two thousand years ago.

What we see today has always been happening. It's not new. It may seem new because we are the ones feeling it and living it, and it's happening to us. Furthermore, social media is amplifying everything to an extent that has never been seen before in history. When somebody stubs their toe, they tell the world. Suddenly it feels as if toe stubbing is a new epidemic, although in reality, it's not.

Yes, people are going through some difficult things, but in America, we went through the Civil War and the Great Depression. We have seen many grim things around the world. I've gone to countries that have suffered savage histories that have torn them apart.

This idea of division is not new, but what do we do about it? We realize the real division is between the individual and what I call *Divinity*. Ho'oponopono refers to God, sometimes to gods in the plural. Dr. Hew Len often called it the *Great Something*, the *Great Mystery*, the *Divine*.

The individual feels separate from the Divine. When we feel separate from Source, we feel vulnerable: we've got no protection; we're here on the planet all by ourselves. Whatever instigates fear in us—whether it's the newspapers, the media, Facebook, Instagram—seems ready to take target practice by sending negativity to us. As long as we feel separate, we are going to feel the emotional impact of that negativity, and it's going to hurt.

How does ho'oponopono help? In Hawaiian—the language the word comes from—it means *to make right*. Ho'oponopono is to make right. It is to correct a perception—the perceptions we have about life, politics, other people, and the social world. Those perceptions are creating the very thing we're complaining about. This is a deep and complicated issue, and I'm going to unravel it in this book.

My book *Zero Limits* came out in 2007. It has been traveling around the world, creating its own following. In 2013, the follow-up book, *At Zero*, appeared. Because of those books, I have heard from people who have used ho'oponopono for everything from healing their pets to healing relationships with their families. I've heard of people using it to increase their wealth and their prosperity and to meet their sales quotas. At this point, I personally have been using it for around fifteen years.

Here are the four basic phrases of ho'oponopono:

I love you.

I'm sorry.

Please forgive me.

Thank you.

These four sentences make up the background voice in my head. Why is it going on? Why do I want it? In the invocation at the beginning of this chapter, I was asking Divinity to cleanse me so that I can be purely in this moment to hear the voice of the Divine. The more I can hear the voice of the Divine, the less I'll be separate, the less division there'll be, and the more I can channel inspiration through this book to help people.

To put it bluntly, ho'oponopono is the road out of hell. Let me put that in perspective. I have studied many philosophies. I was in the movie *The Secret*, which is about the law of attraction, positive thinking, and mind power. Feel-good statements, such as the ones from ancient Stoicism and its most famous proponent, the Roman emperor Marcus Aurelius, can get you through the day. From that perspective, thank God for them, because there are times when we need to get through the day with some sort of statement of support, the old "You can do it." Marcus Aurelius said, "If you can endure it, then endure it." But at a certain point, much of that encouragement becomes impotent. Ho'oponopono can wipe away the need for those statements.

A lot of our reality is cocreated. We're doing it from the inside out. Most of us don't know that; most of us have never even heard this idea before. Even when we do hear it—"Hey, you've cocreated your own reality"—we'll argue about it, we'll dismiss it, we'll fight it, we'll resist hearing it in any way, shape, or form.

Ho'oponopono teaches us to take responsibility for our part in the creation of the very reality we're complaining about. Once we take responsibility for it, we use ho'oponopono. In addition to the four statements, there are many techniques that will help clean up the part of us that created it in the first place.

We use *I love you, I'm sorry, please forgive me, thank you* to clean up the unconscious beliefs, the part of our system that, hidden in the shadows, has been creating our program. We delete that program with ho'oponopono. We're then free of it. We won't create it again.

In the late 1970s in Dallas, I was homeless and went through poverty for around ten years. Even though I had a book published in 1984. It came out of the sky and went back into the sky; it was just a blip. Nothing happened because of it. I was still broke, still unknown.

Slowly, being persistent, working on myself, taking care of my beliefs, I started to get books published in the 1990s. As the Internet came along, I got a name for myself as one of the pioneers of Internet marketing. I wrote one of the first books on Internet marketing, called *Cyber Writing*.

Along around 1998, my first audio program, *The Power of Outrageous Marketing*, came out, which was the turning point for me—a cause for great celebration. It made me a little bit better known on the Internet as a marketer, an outrageous marketer and a copywriter.

I still had a spiritual side to me (I had always had it, ever since I was a kid). I was reading Robert Collier's works, metaphysical books, Napoleon Hill's *Think and Grow Rich*, and others along those lines.

I wrote a little book originally called *Spiritual Marketing*. It did very well. *The New York Times* wrote about it. It was a print-on-demand book. A big publisher picked it up. He didn't like the title. We changed it to *The Attractor Factor*. *The Attractor Factor* was one of the first popular books on the law of attraction. A woman from Australia called me up and said, "Hey, I want to make a movie about the law of attraction, and I'd like you to be in it." I'd never been in a movie before, and I thought it was flattering. It was more than flattering. The movie was *The Secret*. *The Secret* changed everybody's life, including mine, and put me on a new career path as a spiritual teacher.

At this point I was still working on myself, still exploring my own spirituality, still trying to unravel the universe. Even though I'd learned about Internet marketing, copywriting, spirituality, Robert Collier, the law of attraction, about the Secret, I still wasn't done. I wasn't quite satisfied. Something seemed to be missing. This is where I learned about ho'oponopono. At first I dismissed it because I thought, "This is too crazy. This is too ridiculous. How do I say a few phrases inside myself and I change other people? I can change the planet?"

Of course, there's the famous story, which I told in *Zero Limits*, about the therapist (Dr. Hew Len) who helped heal an entire ward of mentally ill criminals with ho'oponopono. How is that possible? I thought it was crazy.

It took me a whole year to accept the possibility that ho'oponopono could make a difference. Then I dived in deep and wrote *Zero Limits*. It came out in 2007—about the same time as *The Secret*. Ironically, just as the movie *The Secret* was making me famous for the law of attraction, I was losing interest in it, because ho'oponopono was taking the lead. I was also unraveling the stages of consciousness, realizing that the Secret and the law of attraction are actually at the lower level of consciousness. If you go up a level, you go to zero limits—and that's where ho'oponopono is.

As I was practicing this, I became a different person; less driven, more inspired; less goal-oriented, more inspiration-oriented; less going for what my ego wanted and paying more attention to what I was being told to do by what I call the *Great Something*, or what Dr. Hew Len calls *Divinity*. There was a profound internal shift in my life.

I am still discovering more about ho'oponopono, still researching it, and also being inspired by the Divine, which is the whole reason for the fifth phrase. The fifth phrase came from direct inspiration. (I will talk about the fifth phrase in chapter 4.)

The unconscious mind is full of limitations, programming, and belief systems—a mental paradigm that the conscious mind isn't aware of. This unconscious mind is living out and acting out through the physical body.

The late Dr. John Sarno, a professor of rehabilitation medicine who specialized in back problems, discovered that they are actually suppressed rage. Sufferers would not even look angry; they would be among the most calm-looking people you would ever meet anywhere. That was a trick of the unconscious, which was protecting that person from feeling rage, thinking, "This person can't handle that kind of an emotional overload, so let's express this ache inside at the weakest point in the body." In Dr. Sarno's cases, it was the back. It had nothing to do with injuries. It had nothing to do with slipped disks, because there were people with slipped disks who did not have pain. Dr. Sarno found that it was the unconscious mind trying to express itself.

What does this have to do with ho'oponopono? Ho'oponopono is designed to find and erase the beliefs in the unconscious mind that are causing the health problem. Many people have been using ho'oponopono for everything from Lyme disease, to Crohn's disease, to cancer, and to some of the most mysterious and persistent ailments out there.

A few years ago, I, along with the rest of my family, was called in because my mother was put in intensive care in an Ohio hospital. We were told that this was the end.

In the intensive care unit, there were only two or three people, and the other two died while I was there. I was looking at my mother, and all kinds of emotions were going through my body—anger, at her, at myself, at God. Why was this happening? I was trying to find somebody to blame. My degrees are in metaphysical science and marketing, not medicine, so what was I left with? Ho'oponopono.

I sat in the chair beside her bed. The rest of the family was in the room, all doing their own grieving. Sitting there, I was saying silently, *I love you, I'm sorry, please for-*

give me, thank you over and over. I wasn't doing it to make her well; I was doing it to bring some sense of peace to me.

This is one reason ho'oponopono is around—to help you find your own tranquility and serenity. When you get there, the outer world can change in response. I kept working on myself until I got to the point where I was more or less at peace. I was not 100 percent at peace, but I was enough so that I thought, "I'm OK now." Then the doctors and nurses said we all had to leave.

The next day I got a phone call. My mother was feeling better and wanted to go home. She did go home, where she lived for the next three years.

Did the ho'oponopono heal her? It's based on the principle that the outer is actually a mirror reflection of the inner you. Seeing my mother on the outside was, in a way, looking at an illusion. As the Buddhists say, life's all an illusion anyway; we just think it's there. What I see outside is actually being projected from inside me. If I take care of whatever is in me that is not at peace and find serenity, I can influence my own illusion. In this particular case, it appeared to work that way.

I've just described a very powerful emotional experience for me individually. So how can ho'oponopono help address some of these emotional issues in our culture?

In my opinion, ho'oponopono actually works better, faster, and more deeply when it's dealing with an emotion, because emotion has fire to it; it grabs your attention. It's one thing to say, "My foot hurts." It's another thing to say, "I am feeling suicidal." When you feel that raw emotion, don't hide from it; actually step into it. Honor it, hone it, hug it, and say the four phrases, including, as I'll show later, the fifth phrase.

When you practice it, ho'oponopono is going to feel and become alive. You're igniting it with emotion. It will go to find out where the emotion is coming from. It is being triggered by a thought, most likely a memory. As a rule, when people are feeling overwhelming emotion, it's being stemmed by some memory. In ho'oponopono, you come either from memory or from inspiration.

For 99.99 percent of us, we're coming from memory. Everything reminds us of something else. We're not in the moment. We're not in the now, with the purity of realizing that this is an uninterrupted, unrepeatable miracle. Most of us bring in baggage.

When you're feeling that emotion, whatever it happens to be, there is, in my estimation, a need to look at where it's coming from. Where was the first root cause of this? As you're looking for it, all you need to do is say, *I love you, I'm sorry, please forgive me, thank you* as a kind of mantra, prayer, or petition. You say it inside yourself while you feel the emotion. You say it to God, to Nature, to Gaia, to the Great Something, the Great Mystery. Islam says there are ninety-nine names of God; probably there are many more. Dr. Hew Len calls it Divinity.

You're petitioning Divinity to unravel, release, clear, and remove that emotion. Ho'oponopono is used for emotional as well as physical ailments. Fill in the blank: what's going on with you that you don't like? Write it down. Now do ho'oponopono on it, because that's how effective it is. You're working with the Divine, which has no limits, to get to a place of peace.

Ho'oponopono is all about integration, wholeness, peace—also about control. Many people are searching for it without realizing that they are in more control than they realize. Many people, when they feel a physical or emotional problem, feel out of control. They feel things are happening to them. They feel a sense of chaos, resulting in sleep issues, stress, physical problems, problems with family and relationships. They want something to help them get control.

Conventional philosophies often encourage us to regain control of our lives: control this disease by wiping it out; control your relationships and your intentions.

Ho'oponopono heals these problems, but not necessarily from a standpoint of gaining more control. In fact, part of the problem is thinking you have control to begin with, because ultimately you don't. That's also one mistake made by the law of attraction movement: you *do* have control, but you don't have total control. You have more than you ever imagined, but you're not in charge. You're not God. You may be a god, but you're not *the* God. At the same time, you have enough control to select things that can be useful to you.

I had some exercise equipment arrive recently, and it was packed in such a way that I needed a crescent wrench to put it together. I don't have a crescent wrench. I am not a tool guy; I don't build things, but I needed a crescent wrench, so I knew to go and get one. Then I was able to unpack the box and assemble the equipment.

Ho'oponopono is a kind of a crescent wrench. You use it to open up whatever is blocking you right now so you can get to the gift, to whatever is for you next. I don't want to be married to ho'oponopono or limited by it. I want to use ho'oponopono like a tool that is available to free me and help me go to the next stage.

Ho'oponopono is a tool, a remarkable, heavenly, God-given tool. It's simple, easy, and free, and it will help you go to the next level. As I've said, it's your road out of hell. Once you're out of hell, you might take a bus, or you might take a plane, or you might do something completely different.

2
The Whiteboard of Your Life

Before we go through an advanced look at ho'opono-pono, let me start with the concept of the whiteboard of your life. This was an inspired image that came to me after the work I was doing with Dr. Hew Len and my own practice of ho'oponopono.

Dr. Len would use the phrase "being at zero," which furnished the title of my second book on ho'oponopono, *At Zero*. And By *at-zero* he meant you're at that place where you don't have memories interfering with this moment and you can receive inspiration from what he would call Divinity. At zero, there are zero distractions, zero beliefs, zero—he would use the word *data*.

Data refers to the baggage of the mind, its stories, its meaning, its beliefs—your mental paradigm. When the data is removed by the practice of ho'oponopono, you can get to a place of purity, what some other cultures might call *enlightenment* or *satori*.

Dr. Hew Len and I called this level *zero limits*. When you're at zero, you don't have any limits, because the limits are man-made; they're mental constructs.

As I became more familiar with the at-zero state, occasionally touching it in meditation or by practicing ho'oponopono, the image of a whiteboard came to mind. When you write on a whiteboard, you can also erase.

I felt that this image came from inspiration. I wasn't really asking for it or doing anything to bring it to me. But one day I had this idea that ho'oponopono was like working with a whiteboard. All of our beliefs are written on the whiteboard, yet the whiteboard is there behind the beliefs; when you erase all of those, there's the purity of the whiteboard. That's like being at zero: you wipe everything off the whiteboard, and there you are, at nothing. That nothing is actually a lot of something, and that something is what we're calling *Divinity*. We're calling it *zero*.

Years ago I gave a talk on ho'oponopono at the Transformational Leadership Council. I had a whiteboard up. I asked everybody, "Tell me your favorite technique for getting the results you want or getting clear or getting healthy or achieving your goals." We spent ten or fifteen minutes hearing from everybody, and I said, "Write them all on the whiteboard." When we were done, you could no longer see the whiteboard. I said, "What happened to the whiteboard?"

All of those techniques, as beneficial as they are at certain moments, are actually in the way of experiencing Divinity. Then as I was talking, I started erasing everything that they had told me off the whiteboard, so that when we were done, there was the whiteboard again.

From the whiteboard you can receive inspiration; you can also deliver a request right to the at-zero state, which is like talking to God.

Once in a seminar someone said, "The whiteboard is a little bit like the Etch A Sketch." As you probably know, the Etch A Sketch is a toy. You sketch on it by turning the knobs, and you can draw all sorts of odd objects and lines and boxes on it. But then you pick it up, turn it over, and shake it, and it's all zeroed out. That's the whiteboard. That's the Etch A Sketch method. Ho'oponopono is the Etch A Sketch, the whiteboard, from the Divine.

In fact you could say that this whiteboard reflects the way we think we are. People put classifications on themselves: "I'm a conservative"; "I'm a liberal"; "I'm a Catholic"; "I'm Jewish"; "I'm extroverted"; "I'm introverted." Most of what we see about ourselves is the markings on the whiteboard rather than the whiteboard itself.

Furthermore, most of this material came from other people. Psychologists have said that most of your sense of self has been ingrained and programmed by the time you're six or seven years old. At that point, you don't really know what's going on in the world yet. You have no sense of your own inner action or involvement with other people or the planet, but you've already made conclusions about yourself. You've labeled yourself, mostly because other people labeled you and you took on those labels.

Thirty or forty years later, you look at yourself and say, "This is who I am. Where did that come from? That actually didn't come from me. It was downloaded from parents and grandparents and uncles and aunts and everybody else when I was growing up." In many ways, this data is an illusion too. It's real to the extent you buy into it and keep repeating it, but you can let go of it.

Motivational speaker Tony Robbins has a great story about a schizophrenic who has certain ailments in one personality and certain talents as another personality. Still another personality doesn't have either that health problem or that talent; it has different ones. Who's the real person? Then there is the case of the famous woman known as Sibyl, who had sixteen different personalities in one individual. You start to wonder what is real when it comes to the personality. Most if not all of it isn't real.

In Russia, I was on the same stage with educator Dr. Joe Dispenza. Joe is doing a lot of work teaching people that you have to break the habit of being yourself. In fact, that's the title of one of his books: *Break the Habit of Being Yourself.*

How do you do that? The first assumption is you're not whatever you think you are. Once you can grasp that, you can work with the second premise: who would you like to be?

Ho'oponopono works in those all different areas. It's an ancient Hawaiian system that has evolved over the years, although it wasn't the kind of ho'oponopono we practice today. The earlier version, which is still around, was a group problem solving technique, usually done with a tribe or a family. It was led by an elder, a father figure or therapist who would hear the problem. Then he would have all the different people involved do their repentance, do their "I'm sorries" and "Please forgive mes."

The version of ho'oponopono I'm discussing here came from Morrnah Simeona (1913–92), who was a kahuna, a Hawaiian shaman, and was considered to be enlightened. She taught Dr. Hew Len. She was receiving inspiration from Divinity: she kept going to the whiteboard, going to zero, and she could receive information.

In 1980, Morrnah announced to the world, "You don't need all those people, because you *are* all those people. They're all a reflection of you. In a way they're parts of you. You can do that group technique inside yourself by talking to Divinity and repeating *I love you, I'm sorry, please forgive me, thank you.*"

People may wonder whether we really have the power to wipe away what passes for ourselves and write on the whiteboard what we wish. Is it really that simple? What about issues that are tied to our genes over which we have no control? Some people say, "I have a genetic inheritance of intelligence," or "I have a genetic inheritance of this disease." They may think that certain immutable realities of life have been written on our whiteboard.

A lot of people believe these things. In fact that's the key: belief. It is true as long as you believe it. Previously everybody believed that this was obvious: if you have genes going in a certain direction, you're going to go in that direction, because you can't change your genes.

Today scientists are coming back with hard evidence saying you are not confined to your genes; you are not confined to some predestined way of living. Biologists like Bruce Lipton say that that's not true at all. You are not confined to your genes. You actually turn on and off your genes depending on your state of consciousness. Other experts, like Dr. Joe Dispenza, say the same thing. You have genes inside, waiting, almost, for orders.

These new scientists have been looking at the backgrounds of people who have gone through cancer. Often they find that the patients have gone through traumatic experiences. Some scientists regard the disease as an attempt at conflict resolution: something occurred that the person hasn't been able to resolve. A mental conflict is going on inside them, so they go into a kind of despair. The body, feeling this darkness, turns on the cells that turn on cancer.

By the same token, you can turn these cells off. This is when Dr. Joe Dispenza teaches people to go into a state of gratitude, a state of love. In essence, you're going to Source—the source of life. If you go there mentally, spiritually, and emotionally, you can experience love and turn on your own healing essence.

I remember thinking a while back, is there really anything impossible? Is there really anything we can't do? I couldn't come up with anything. We may feel it's impossible, but right now somebody is working on it or has already proved that it's possible. There are people working with time travel. Some scientists are saying, "We've done these experiments. We've been able to go backwards or forwards only by two seconds, but two seconds is the beginning in proving time travel is possible."

Once I wrote a blog post about my book *Anything Is Possible*. Somebody flippantly wrote back and said, "What about limb regeneration?"

At first I thought, "Go for some of your dreams in your life. Why would you go for an extreme example just to argue with me?" But then I thought, "Maybe they have a point." I did some research and found that scientists in fact are regenerating limbs in humans. Science itself is proving that we are not confined to a destiny that we can't change. And ho'oponopono puts us back in, if not the driver's seat, at least the passenger's cocreation seat. From there, from the whiteboard, from at-zero, where there are no limits, you can have do or be whatever you want.

Having read this, you may be wondering how you could get a sense of this whiteboard on a daily basis and start tapping into these possibilities.

One of the first and the easiest techniques is pausing with awareness. We live in busy times. We often feel chained to our own phones, so we don't have time to relax, to be at peace, to calm down. We need to shake the Etch A Sketch: turn everything off and get back to zero. Every hour (or at least once a day), take thirty seconds or a minute, turn the phone off and put it aside. Do it as a kind of a meditation, and ask yourself, "Am I my thoughts?"

If you pause long enough, you're going to hear the answer: "Yeah, I'm my thoughts." But what's behind that? What's behind the voice that just said that? You are witnessing your thoughts. If you're witnessing your thoughts, you're not your thoughts. You're this witness; you're the spy on your own thoughts.

The same thing is true of your emotions. What are you feeling? Maybe it was a rough day; maybe you're aggravated, frustrated, tired, grieving.

Again, you can spy on your emotions, describe them, report on them. Therefore you are not your emotions. This is another clue to take you to at-zero—to the whiteboard.

The third element is the body itself. Really get into the body, realizing not "I am a body" but "I'm wearing a body." You're, again, a spy from the inside of your body, observing what's going on: you don't feel good, your back hurts, or your foot hurts. You're reporting on your body; therefore you and the body are separate.

Although this practice takes some time to describe, it doesn't have to take long to do. You're behind the wheel of the car. Before you go into an appointment, you stop. You take a deep breath, which pulls you into your body. You realize that this body is like a suit. It's my meat suit, it's my astronaut suit, and I'm in it. Then I notice my feelings and I notice, OK, I have feelings, but I'm not these feelings, which means I'm detached from them, or could be. The same with my thoughts: I'm narrating all of this, but there's a part of me that's a witness to it.

The closer we can get to this witness, the closer we are to zero, the closer we are to shaking the Etch A Sketch, the closer we are to a blank whiteboard. When we're sitting there, worried, replaying everything in our head, and feeling the resulting emotions, we are miles away; we have sprinted way past zero. We're not there anymore. We want to pause, reflect, take a deep breath, and come back.

This practice is just like any habit: we have to remind ourselves to do it. When I first learned ho'oponopono, I didn't have the four phrases memorized. (In fact, memorization is one of my weakest skills; I'm still working on it.) I had to write them down. I wrote them down on little stickies and put them on the computer, on the refrigerator, in the bathroom, on the dashboard. For a while I wrote them on my hand in ink. I saw a woman recently who had the four phrases tattooed on her arm. You do whatever it takes.

The first time you start using those phrases (or the fifth phrase, when we get to it), it will be awkward and uncomfortable, because it's the beginning of a new habit. The habits you already have are easy and unconscious. You can do them all the time; you can do them until you die, because you already set up that memory path in your brain. But when you start a new habit, like pausing every day and putting the phone aside, you might need a reminder.

I use my phone for a lot of different things, including setting a timer on it to turn the phone itself off. I'll decide that at 3:00 p.m., I'm going to do a little gratitude meditation. I set the phone to remind me to do that. Then: "Thank you, phone. You are now off." You can use the devil to push the devil away.

You can even pause to experience the whiteboard when reading this book.

Let me emphasize an important point here. In ho'opo-nopono, there's an underlying belief that there is Divinity, that there is a God, that there is something at zero or at the whiteboard. Not only is it alive, but it is an intelligent being of some sort. You may want take away the emotions surrounding the word *God* and just say, "This is Nature," as the Stoics did. When you're at zero, you are at your purest, because you're coming from Source, and this is natural.

The ancient Hawaiians had many gods because they were afraid. They were living with volcanoes around them, with possible floods and starvation. They had more than one god, because they thought they needed all the help they could get.

In the ho'oponopono of Dr. Hew Len, it's more of a single source, which he called Divinity. Joseph Camp-bell called it the Great Mystery; I call it the Great Something. I'm not sure we'll ever all agree on what to call it, but there is something we can all agree is bigger than us. Some people just call it a higher power. We can tap into that and use it as an ally, as a cocreative force.

When people look at their lives even logically, they have to admit something's going on that is keeping my heart beating, my body moving, my breathing working, my lungs working. I'm not doing all of that. Even if it's a biologically based automated system, where did that come from? Who set it up? Who designed it? Is this truly a grand accident? It seems impossible. I can't even calculate how that would take place.

This leads to another point: where did ho'oponopono come from? Some, including Dr. Hew Len, speculate that it came from other planets. Some say it was from a continent like Atlantis that disappeared a long time ago.

The fundamental point is a belief in some greater power that you tap into with ho'oponopono. When you're saying the four phrases, you're saying them to something, to someone, to some sort of energy. As you do, you're making a request; you're basically saying, "I don't feel so well; I don't even know why. My stomach's upset. It's been that way for a long time. I need healing." Usually you don't even know what the reason is.

You're delivering this petition to this Source, again with faith, trusting it's going to be resolved. That's the first level here. There's faith involved. I wear a ring. It's twenty-five hundred years old, from ancient Italy. It's got the word *fidem* on it. *Fidem* is Latin for *faith*.

I used not to wear it, but Dr. Hew Len asked to see it. I took it off and put it in his palm. He kept it in his palm for a moment, and then he said, "You need to wear it, and wear it all the time. That is your reminder of faith."

I am telling this story to help people realize that they too need to have faith. When people say ho'oponopono doesn't work, often they haven't done it long enough to see the results; they're blind to what is working that they're not able to see.

I've heard this in other fields. When the movie *The Secret* came out, a lot of people weren't very nice. They'd walk up and say, "It's bogus; it doesn't work."

One woman said, "Affirmations don't work."

"You do know that's an affirmation, right?" I said.

To say "Affirmations don't work" is affirming that affirmations don't work, which means they work. A lot of people denounce things that are actually working, although they may not have the clarity or patience to see it. Maybe they need a coach or mentor to point it out to them.

Dr. Hew Len often said, "If you could see all that was being changed when you did ho'oponopono, you would never, ever stop."

Things are being rearranged behind the scenes. It's like a snowplow in the middle of the night. We're sleeping in our comfy beds, but it's snowing. Yet somehow, when you get up in the morning, the roads are clear. Who did that?

Ho'oponopono is like the snowplows and street sweepers that come out at night. They've paved your way to make your life easier, but you didn't see them do it. You didn't see what ho'oponopono moved out of the way to get you to the next day.

Again, this is on faith; this is on trust. Sometimes I practice a tough love approach and say, "Look, it doesn't cost you anything. How hard is it to say, *I love you, I'm sorry, please forgive me, thank you*?"

If you don't want to say the four phrases, or you don't understand why you're saying them, just pick one. Ho'oponopono teacher Mabel Katz says, "If you just said *thank you* all the time, you would change yourself." Personally, I say, *I love you.*

Imagine walking through your life silently saying, "I love you." At first you might think, "Yeah. I don't really love you." But as you say it over and over again, your internal state will catch up. Scientists say we are sending out invisible signals that other people feel. When we walk into a party, we get a sense of the different people there; we want to go to some, and we want to stay away from others. We're not reading the situation logically; we're reading it unconsciously. When we say *I love you* over and over again, we send out an *I love you* signal, which changes everything.

A lot of people have problems saying, *Please forgive me.* But at one point a Christian friend told me, "When Jesus healed people, he didn't walk up and say, 'You are healed.' The first thing he said was, 'You are forgiven.'" Forgiveness was necessary before the miracle could happen.

Ho'oponopono—which is somewhat Christian-influenced—does include the phrase *Please forgive me.* But it's not referring to a punishment. It's not implying that you did something wrong. It's referring to the fact that you were unconscious: unconscious of your own beliefs, your programming, or where the programming came from.

For some people who are reading this book, this might be a stark shake of reality. It's like grabbing them, shaking them, and saying, "Here's what's really going on in your life, although you never saw it before. You never understood it before." When you actually understand this, you might turn to the Divine and say, "Please forgive me. I had no idea." That's where that phrase came from.

I've been asked how the ho'oponopono process differs from traditional success concepts like goal setting, visualization, affirmations, and neurolinguistic programming (NLP). We could say that these techniques generally work on the level of thought and emotion, not on the level of zero or the Great Something. In other words, these techniques speak to the markings on the whiteboard, but not the whiteboard itself.

One of my favorite teachers, Arnold Patent, once said that we don't create abundance; we create limitations. Ho'oponopono removes the limitations.

I was in Russia recently, and people were talking about creating abundance. They asked, "When we've removed all these limiting beliefs, what do we install? How do we install the new beliefs that will bring in the money we need?" I replied, "You don't install them; you don't need to install them." As Arnold Patent suggested, remove the limitations, and what do you have? Abundance.

What limitations does ho'oponopono remove? The negative beliefs, the limiting beliefs, the paradigms we grew up with, the scarcity mindset we probably inherited. With ho'oponopono, we remove those limitations, but we don't need to install anything afterwards.

Dr. Hew Len often emphasized that you don't need intentions; you don't need goals; you don't need goal setting; you don't need to tell the Divine what to do. The Divine knows what to do, and the Divine will tell you what you need to do when you need to know it. With Divinity, you're on a need to know basis.

At the same time, even to say that you don't need intentions is kind of an intention. To say, "I want the Divine to lead the way" is an intention.

This can be a little tricky. For me, using traditional goal setting techniques to tell the Divine what to do will backfire, because we're acting as if we know better than the Divine. But in fact I've just got a little ego that's trying to make its way through life. I don't know the universe in all its ebb and flow or all the people and their aspirations and stories. I have no way of sorting through all that. It's easier for me to go to the Divine and say, "You know what? You're smarter than me. You tell me what to do next. You inspire me."

I used to talk about intentions, but intentions are for wimps. They come from my ego. My ego is going to base its intentions on what it already believes is possible, which is based on the past—what I heard, what I read, what I saw, what I believe. I prefer inspirations. Inspirations come right from the whiteboard, from the zero state, from Source, and they may blow my mind. They may tell me to do or say something that I'd never thought of. I'd rather go with inspiration, which in a sense is marching orders from the Divine, than with my ego. My ego should serve the Divine and not the other way around.

Let me conclude this chapter by outlining some of the foundational principles behind ho'oponopono as taught by Dr. Hew Len.

First, *everything is alive*. That is a traditional Hawaiian way of looking at life. It's found in other cultures, but it was new to me. When Dr. Hew Len talked about everything being alive, at first I thought he meant my cat, my dog, my relatives, and so forth—but no. He meant the furniture, the walls, the floor, the chairs, the carpet—everything.

Once when we did an event—I believe it was in Austin, Texas—I took Dr. Hew Len to the hotel to examine the event room beforehand. He went into the room, and he wanted to talk to it, which I thought was pretty bizarre (although at that point, all of ho'oponopono was pretty bizarre). He walked to the walls and touched them. He looked at me and said, "The walls are sad."

"The walls are sad? Why are they sad? They're freaking walls!"

"There have been so many people who have come and gone, but none have shown appreciation for the walls holding up the building and making this room possible," Dr. Hew Len replied.

He asked me to talk to the floor. "Just talk to the floor," he said. "There's no right or wrong. What do you think it's saying?"

I looked at it, and honestly, the floor was not talking to me.

"No," said Dr. Hew Len, "just allow your intuition. Just look at the floor and pretend that it's talking to you. What might it be saying?"

"Well," I said, "it's probably heavily trafficked. So it's worn thin. It's probably feeling uncomfortable, probably unappreciated, a little bit like the wall."

"Yeah," said Dr. Hew Len.

Dr. Hew Len talked to the chairs and then to the room as a whole. He named it Sheila. The whole story is in my book *Zero Limits*.

When I started to entertain the idea that everything is alive, I had a newfound respect for the planet. It's not just me, my dog, my cat, and my relatives. We're all in this together. Everything, the rocks, the water, the sand—everything that you can think of, everything you can name—is part of the whole.

The ancient Hawaiians knew this. The ancient Stoics, such as Marcus Aurelius and Epictetus, also treated the planet as alive. They didn't think it was us against something else. We are all in this together.

The second principle is *everything is a mirror.* This also came from Morrnah when in 1980 she introduced the modernized version of self-identity ho'oponopono, as she called it. She was saying that everything is a mirror of what's going on inside of you. The old version of ho'oponopono had the elder and the family members get together in a kind of a tribal group therapy. But, said Morrnah, all of those people are really reflecting parts of you. If you do the work of finding peace with and asking for forgiveness from those parts within you, you will return to the place of serenity. You'll get to tranquility, and you can let go of trying to manipulate the outer world.

This is not news, because Carl Jung and other proponents of depth psychology taught that we have a shadow side in our unconscious mind. The unconscious is projecting that shadow side outside, onto other people. If we want to change other people, we don't work on them; we work on ourselves. When we work on ourselves and get to a place of peace, forgiveness, and neutrality, lo and behold, they will look as if they've changed, but what really changed was you.

My favorite story about this is about how Dr. Hew Len helped heal an entire ward of mentally ill criminals at the state mental hospital in Hawaii. Without telling anybody else there, he used ho'oponopono.

The hospital needed to have a licensed doctor. All of the other ones had quit, because it was a hellish place. People would walk down the hallways with their backs against the wall, because they might be attacked. The inmates were so violent that they needed to be sedated or shackled.

Dr. Hew Len went there, but he did not work on the inmates. He worked on himself. He would look at their files and he would find out that they were rapists, murderers, mentally ill criminals. Whatever he felt inside himself—embarrassment, sadness, anger, rage, whatever—he would say, *I love you, I'm sorry, please forgive me, thank you.* He would clean on it. He was not working with those people. He was not cleaning or clearing on them; he wasn't doing traditional therapy. He was saying in effect that those people were illusions; they were mirror projections of what was in him. As he cleaned up himself, they got better. That's what made ho'oponopono world-famous.

When I heard it, I said, "If this is true, we've got to tell the world, because it has so many implications." I interviewed Dr. Hew Len, and I found the social workers that were there at the time. I did all of that as a good journalist in order to write the first book on ho'oponopono.

The premise is that the rest of the world is a mirror. Many people have said, "I had a problem with my boss, I had a problem with my employee, with my sister, my parents," whatever it was. They learned ho'oponopono. Instead of addressing the problem with the people involved, they addressed what they were feeling inside themselves. They'd say, *I love you, I'm sorry, please forgive me, thank you.* They were making a petition to the Great Something to erase these patterns so they could get back to zero. They wanted to be at zero inside themselves; when they got there, the other people changed.

Why? Because these other people were reflecting what was inside of them. Jung says that if you're upset at other people, it's because they remind you of a part of you that you don't want to accept. If you see somebody else doing what others might call irritating behavior and you don't have that reflection in you, you just look at them with neutrality. You don't say they're good or bad. That issue is no longer there.

This second premise is fundamental to ho'opono-pono, as it is to many psychologies: *if you want to change something, you change you.* Trying to change others is like looking in the mirror and putting makeup on it, or trying to shave the mirror rather than shaving yourself.

The third premise of ho'oponopono is *everything can change.* At one of our Zero Limits events, a person in the audience stood up and said, "Life is like this giant, long, majestic painting, and everything is being painted as we move through life. Everything seems as if it's already been predestined, but it wasn't."

Dr. Hew Len stood up and said, "And as you clean, you change the painting," and he sat down.

Dr. Hew Len was at zero. As he heard the audience member speak, something out of the purity of space hit within him. He stood up, made his contribution, and sat down. He'd gotten marching orders from the Divine.

The rest of us thought, "Oh my God! Yes, there is a painting, but we're the ones painting it. And as we do ho'oponopono, we're changing the painting. It's mind-blowing."

We don't know anything about life. There is such an incomprehensible mystery to the universe that no scientists are going to figure it out and say, "Here's what it's all about." They're not going to get to that, because it is too big to wrestle to the ground.

What are we left with? We're left with faith. We're left with being in the moment. As we're cleaning, we're also changing the painting.

We don't understand life. Life is a giant mystery. But behind the mystery is this essence, this witness that we're part of. When we go into the witness of ourselves, when we go into the at-zero state, where we erase everything from the whiteboard, we are at that place of witnessing. That witness in us is God, the Divine.

In his mystical classic *The Practice of the Presence of God*, Brother Lawrence said to pretend that you were in God's presence in every moment. If you really take that on, God is with you right now. Call it the Divine, call it the witness, call it Gaia, call it what you like. If you really come from that place, you start to move into living the miracle. You start to live from the place of zero limits and the whiteboard, and you start to come from a place where inspiration can whisper to you. When it does, brace yourself for magic and miracles, because that's what happens.

3

The Four Phrases
of Ho'oponopono

Before I go any further, let me review the origin of ho'oponopono, my meeting with Dr. Hew Len, and the first four phrases.

I've already told a little bit of the story of Dr. Hew Len. I heard of the strange therapist who helped heal an entire ward of mentally ill criminals. Of course, when I first heard it, I dismissed it; that's how smart I am. I was skeptical and cautious, but I kept hearing about the story. A year later, I thought, "If this is true, the world needs to know." I wanted to find out if it was true, and I needed to find the therapist.

This was around 2003 or 2004. There was no material on Dr. Hew Len, the mental hospital, or ho'oponopono. I Googled all over the place; there was nothing. I even hired a private detective to find the mysterious therapist. He couldn't find him. I kept asking, and I kept shaking trees, and then somebody had a pamphlet that they gave out in the little ho'oponopono workshops they were doing in Hawaii. I found an email address, and I wrote to the person there. One thing led to another, and I found Dr. Hew Len. I called him up. He didn't know me at all. He'd never heard of me or my reputation, but he was very kind. He spent forty-five minutes on the phone with me.

"Tell me about this ho'oponopono," I said.

He said, "All ho'oponopono was designed to do is to make things right."

"How does it work?"

"All you do is clean."

"What does that mean?"

"Cleaning is what you're doing to erase data."

"What's the data?"

It just got more and more confusing, but something intrigued me. I asked him about the story of the hospital: "Did you really help heal those mentally ill criminals?"

"I didn't do it alone," he said, "but yes, I used ho'oponopono."

"I have to know more."

He was doing a workshop in Carlsbad, California, about two weeks later. I said, "I'm coming."

I went. It was just a little seminar room in a hotel. Nothing fancy, nothing mystical about it. There were maybe fifteen people in the room. There was an old, grandfatherly, Hawaiian-looking man wearing a baseball cap. He came over and said he was Dr. Hew Len. He was very relaxed, very laid-back. I liked him instantly.

When Dr. Hew Len began the event, he told story after story. He had no notes; he had nothing to pass out; he had nothing to show on an overhead, no PowerPoints, nothing a traditional speaker might have. He certainly wasn't like a minister, he wasn't standing up there and preaching, but he was talking about the universe. He was talking about Divinity. He was talking about Morrnah, who taught him the four phrases. He recited them and told us, "You just say these to Divinity, and you can change your life. You can change whatever is going on in you."

Everybody was eating up every word he said. I was still being a skeptical journalist: "Prove it to me. Show me something here. Give me something to work with."

Things got even odder at that point, because somebody said, "I'm looking at the wall behind you, Dr. Hew Len, and it looked like it just opened up to be a portal, and some spirits came through."

"What am I doing here?" I was thinking. "What is this place?"

Dr. Hew Len said, "There are spirits coming through, because you gave attention to the portal. Quit giving it attention, and it'll close up and they'll go away."

At this point I didn't know where I was or what I was doing, but I wanted to know more because of the story of how these four phrases helped Dr. Hew Len heal mentally ill criminals. Why couldn't it do for me what it did for you? We're not in a mental institution for the criminally insane. If it helped them, how can it help me with my little everyday problems? That's why I was there. That's what I wanted to know.

As the seminar went on, I heard stories from people who said things that sounded pretty preposterous. One woman said she was sitting in the airport, waiting for a plane that was late. She just started saying, *I love you, I'm sorry, please forgive me, thank you*, on the fact that the plane was late. According to her, because she said this, the plane showed up on time. Again I'm thinking, "This is a wild stretch for my usually open brain." I was having a tough time.

At another point in the seminar, they had us lie on the floor to do a stretch exercise. Dr. Hew Len was walking around, looking at people. He looked at one woman, and he told me, "She's demonstrating the anger of women toward men." I was looking at her. She was just doing a Pilates move. I didn't see anger from women for men. The whole thing was getting confusing to me, and I started to wonder, "What am I here for? He's an eccentric, likable guy, but I'm not getting it."

Dr. Hew Len focused on *I love you, I'm sorry, please forgive me, thank you*. He focused on Morrnah. Although he thought she was crazy when he first met her, he said she was a divine resource from Hawaii. She taught him these phrases. He's spending his life teaching the phrases to other people, including me.

At the end of that seminar, I went to my room in the hotel. I noticed that I had a urinary tract infection. It was weird and uncomfortable. I didn't know what it was there for; I didn't know what was infecting me. I decided to use *I love you, I'm sorry, please forgive me, thank you* on it. I was thinking, "I've got this infection. It feels uncomfortable. I don't know where it came from. I don't know what it's all about, but I love you, I'm sorry, please forgive me, thank you."

At this point, I was just saying the statements. I didn't understand them; I couldn't break them down; I didn't know the reasoning behind them. I didn't know what they would unlock. It was all on faith, on trust. I didn't even have them memorized yet, but I said them over and over.

I went to bed. When I woke up in the morning, the infection was gone. I thought, "Was that a coincidence?" Then I thought, "I wonder if I can create other coincidences by using the same four phrases."

The next day I said to Dr. Hew Len, "You know, this just worked for me, and I'm hearing about it working for other people. This needs to be told in the form of a book. I would like to write it."

"The Divine said somebody else was going to write the book," he said so he couldn't agree for me to do it yet. As time went on, he did agree for me to write the book, which ended up being *Zero Limits*.

Let me go more deeply into those four phrases. First of all, why the four phrases? I don't really know. Morrnah was the person who received them from inspiration. She was considered to be a kahuna. She passed them on to Dr. Hew Len, who passed them on to me. I'm passing them on to everybody else.

Why do the four phrases work at all? What's behind them? How do you unpack them?

To begin with, these four phrases are said internally. You rarely say them out loud. That's one of the first principles. You say them internally, because you're talking to your connection to the Divine. I don't need to say the four phrases to you, because I'm not cleaning or clearing or cleansing you; I'm cleansing *me*. It may be my observation of you or somebody else, but I'm doing it internally.

People always ask, what order do you say them in? In whatever order feels right to you. As I said in a previous chapter, you can just say, *thank you* or *I love you*. You can pick one of the statements. In my opinion, it's more effective to use all four, and there's a reasoning behind this. I say them in whatever order feels right, and that's what I tell people to do. Usually it's in this order: *I love you, I'm sorry, please forgive me, thank you,* but let's break it down.

We say, *Please forgive me,* because as I mentioned in a previous chapter, you've been unconscious of your own programming. You're basically saying, "Please forgive me; I was not aware. I was not cognizant of what was going on in that moment. I wasn't aware of my own belief system. I wasn't aware of my own patterns."

You're not admitting to wrongdoing. You're not admitting anything that you should be guilty for. There isn't anything about soliciting punishment here. You're simply saying, "Hey, please forgive me. I didn't know." That's it.

It's similar with *I'm sorry.* People have problems saying *I'm sorry,* which is very interesting. Recently I had a number of deaths among family and friends. People came to the funeral and they all said, "I'm sorry." Part of me was thinking, "Why are they sorry? They had nothing to do with the death. They didn't cause it. They weren't directly involved, but they're telling me they're sorry."

This is the mindset you want to have when you say, *I'm sorry.* It's like bumping into somebody in a crowded store. Don't you say, "I'm sorry"? What are you really saying? "I'm sorry, I didn't see you there. I'm sorry, I was not conscious in that moment. I'm sorry, I wasn't aware of my own behavior." Whatever it happens to be, you're saying, "I'm sorry, I wasn't aware. Please forgive me. I wasn't thinking."

All of this has a neutrality to it. People have problems when they add their own meanings to it. They say, "I'm sorry because I did wrong," or "Please forgive me, because I'm a bad person." That's not what we're saying. That is not in ho'oponopono. It is "I'm sorry, I made a mistake." It's "Please forgive me, I bumped into you." It's very neutral.

I love *thank you*, because it moves you into a state of gratitude, which I think is one of the most powerful forces on the planet. Just starting to say *thank you* over and over is a window to the miraculous.

There are at least two levels. One is "Thank you for taking care of this problem. Thank you for curing me. Thank you for healing this situation. Thank you for resolving it." The first level is "Thank you for answering this prayer. Thank you for removing whatever the problem was."

The second level is gratitude for being alive. It is the feeling that the universe, the Divine, the whiteboard, the Great Something, is giving you more than you'll ever be able to return. You cannot outgive the universe. You cannot outgive the Divine. The very breath that you take in—you have nothing to do with it, yet that's what keeps you going. *Thank you* moves you into that place of overwhelming gratitude for the gift of life. It's powerful all by itself, which is why Mabel Katz, one popular teacher of ho'oponopono, says, "The only one you really need to say is *thank you*."

I like *I love you*. It's one of those high-vibe statements in its own right. On one level, you're merging with the Divine. You're saying, "I love you, Spirit. I love you, Divine. I love you, Nature. I love you, life." On another level, it's kind of a thank you to be able to say *I love you* to the source of life itself. I'm smiling and feeling warm in my heart to realize that saying *I love you* internally to that connection brings me closer to that connection. The more I can feel or express love as I say *I love you*, the more I merge with it. If there's any word that describes that whiteboard or zero point, it's probably *love*. Saying *I love you* moves me closer to it.

As you can see, *I love you, I'm sorry, please forgive me, thank you* has a lot more behind it than just the four phrases. They're not empty words.

Dr. Hew Len was asked, "Do you have to feel the words when you're saying them? Do you have to feel love when you say, *I love you*? Do you have to feel sorry when you say, *I'm sorry* or *Please forgive me*? Do you have to feel gratitude when you say *Thank you*?" He said, "No. As you say them, the effects will kick in. The more you say them, you will start to feel them. You will start to feel the embodiment of them. The emotions will stir in you as you make those statements."

To my mind, ho'oponopono works better when you do feel love as you say, *I love you* or you feel gratitude when you say, *thank you*. Dr. Hew Len advises just to say them.

You may be able to envision yourself using these phrases around healing physical issues, emotional issues, or relationships. But what about really tragic circumstances? Let's say someone is raped or was abused as a child. Somebody's partner embezzled the funds, and they have lost their life's savings. They may be feeling, "Why do I have to say, *I love you, I'm sorry, please forgive me, thank you*? Why do I need to be forgiven? It's this person that needs to be forgiven. It's this person that did this evil thing to me."

Let's go back to one of the fundamental premises of ho'oponopono: *you are totally responsible for your life.* Dr. Hew Len always asked, "Have you ever noticed that when you have a problem, you are there? You are there."

You are the common denominator in all of your problems. You have something to do with them. As I've already emphasized, when you make the four statements, you're not admitting in any way, shape, or form that you did something wrong. You're saying that maybe you've been unconscious, maybe you weren't thinking, maybe you weren't aware, maybe you were blind to your own programming. Believe me, we all are. We don't understand our own programming. Life is all about awakening. That's what we're all wrestling with—to become more aware and more godlike as we grow into expanded levels of consciousness.

None of this means that while we're still awakening we're responsible in a punishment-oriented way. One therapist in Houston had a brilliant TV commercial: "It is not your fault, but it *is* your responsibility," referring to any problem, anything going on in your life. That's pure ho'oponopono, though I doubt that the therapist ever knew it.

In this case, you're acknowledging that something tragic has happened to you. It's not your fault. That's where I would stop. It's not your fault, but it is your responsibility.

One of my all-time favorite movies is *Good Will Hunting*. There's an incredible scene where Robin Williams, who plays a therapist, is talking to the hero, played by Matt Damon. He's become a tough guy trying to hide a hurt little kid within himself because of all the abuse he's taken—being beaten by his father, having cigars put out on his body. The therapist tells him, "It's not your fault, everything you've gone through."

I have watched this movie many times, and I've counted the number of times he says this. Eleven times, Robin Williams says, "It is not your fault. It is not your fault. It is not your fault."

We've all had challenges, in many cases traumas. It is not your fault, but it is your responsibility to do something about it. We don't know what elements came into play to make a situation happen, whatever the dastardly deed might have been, but here we are. We've got post-traumatic stress disorder (PTSD). We've got illness. We've got something we have to wrestle with, something we want to heal. All right: in this moment, I take responsibility for it. I'm going to do something about it.

The first level of doing something about it is *I love you, I'm sorry, please forgive me, thank you.* It is not saying that you are trying to forgive or punish yourself or somebody else. You're not coming from that old world mentality. Ho'oponopono brings a new, spiritual, higher-level view of life. Yes, you're taking responsibility, but you're taking it to free yourself. That's the beauty of this practice—to heal yourself and free yourself. As you do, maybe the other people involved will change. We don't really know, but that's not the purpose. The purpose is to change *you*, much as Dr. Hew Len in the mental hospital did the practice to change himself. As he felt better looking at the inmates' records, with some sort of incomprehensible magic that I don't understand and can't explain, they started to get better.

When my mother was dying in intensive care, I was working on *me*, and the next day she got better. I don't understand it. I was doing it to bring myself to a state of serenity and tranquility and forgiveness, to a state of love. That's why we're doing all of this, even in tragic circumstances.

In terms of integrating ho'oponopono into your daily life, the old world part of me, which is used to being in the self-help movement, wants to give you to-dos, tasks, assignments and say, "Start a journal," "Do this every day at three o'clock," or "Do it first thing in the morning."

Then there's the other part of me, the new world part, which is heavily influenced by ho'oponopono and says, "Do what feels right to you."

Ho'oponopono claims that you come either from memory or from inspiration. If we come from memory, we think, "What things have worked for me before. Oh, when I made a to-do list, that worked for me. When I set up my phone to set a reminder beep off, that worked for me." That's the memory approach. It's one way of going through life.

The inspiration approach would be more like, "Let's just make the time open within ourselves and see what the Divine says." The Divine might have some original, completely surprising, off-the-wall suggestion. That would be the thing to do.

My general answer is a blend of both. People for whom this practice is brand-new may need to treat it like a meditation. Make time to meditate every day. I don't know if that's nine in the morning or nine in the evening; you pick. Maybe take a ten- or twenty-minute time for meditation, but make it *I love you, I'm sorry, please forgive me, thank you.* Use it on whatever is going on in your life in this moment.

Also make time for nothing. Maybe at the end of your practice, you allow thirty seconds or a minute of silence.

That's like taking your phone off the hook in order to receive. You could receive the inspiration you need.

Recently I heard a definition of intuition: it is the whisper of the gods. I thought, "Wow, how cool is that?" but you've got to be silent to hear a whisper, even if it's a whisper from the gods. You've got to shut up to hear it.

In the beginning, maybe the best advice is to do a blend: a little bit of "Let's start a new habit and do ho'oponopono once a day," and a little bit of "Let's make some silence at the end of the ho'oponopono to receive some guidance."

Dr. Hew Len said to do this practice all the time. Never stop. First it's a new habit, but once it's ingrained and takes over in your mind, it works all the time. It becomes automatic, like a default setting. I've got it set to that channel, and I'm listening to *I love you, I'm sorry, please forgive me, thank you* every moment.

Here's another tip. A lot of people either use the four phrases recorded by me and let it play on a loop or make a recording for themselves. Get out your iPhone or whatever computer you're using and make a twenty-minute audio in your own voice, repeating *I love you, I'm sorry, please forgive me, thank you*. Maybe pace it out a little bit, make it slow and gentle, but let it be your voice. Then play that all the time. Put it on a background loop and let it play in your office or while you're walking, working out, driving, or doing any number of things. Let it be almost subliminal. Let it be a whisper in the background. That way you'll be getting the effects of ho'oponopono in your own voice until it becomes automatic in your mind.

Let's go back to the concept of cleaning. It's like cleaning the dust off of your computer screen, or cleaning your house. You need to do regularly, because if you don't, eventually everything reverts to disorder.

We're cleaning on the limitations in our own mind, the seen and the unseen, the conscious and the subconscious. We're cleaning and clearing everything. That's the purpose of ho'oponopono. As Dr. Hew Len says, our purpose to be here so we can hear the Divine.

When Dr. Hew Len came to the city I was living in, we were writing the book *Zero Limits*. I left him in his room for a while and ran some errands. When I came back a few hours later, I asked what he had been doing. He said he was watching TV. I thought, "That was rare." I was thinking of him as an incredible enlightened guru, and he was in his room watching television. That's not what I thought he would do. I said, "Really? What were you watching?"

"The news," he said.

"The news?" I tell the world to turn off the news. Quit paying attention to the news. The news is anti-law of attraction. It's be the most harmful thing to put in your head. Yet here he was, watching the news. Why?

He said, "Because as it triggers me, I clean on what's being triggered."

I realized it was a self-help technique. It was his way of continuing spiritual cleaning. You're cleaning on everything that triggers you, whether it's on TV, at the bus stop, or in line at the coffee shop—everything that angers you, upsets you, throws you out of balance.

When you're stuck in traffic and somebody pulls out in front of you, you yell at them because you were triggered. Some belief came up that said, "That person is in the wrong. That person's harming me. That person's a threat to me. That person is a—" fill in the blank. You're cleaning on everything that triggers you.

When you're trying to make sales in your business and people aren't buying, you start grumbling, you pound the table and say, "It's the economy. It's the president. It's the political system. It's my parents. It's the competition." Before you start blaming all of them, clean on that trigger. Everything that takes you away from your moment-by-moment happiness is a trigger that can be cleaned and cleared. That's the data of the mind. Those are beliefs. Those are limitations. Those are mindsets. Those are paradigms, most of which you inherited from limited-thinking people who had them and didn't even know they did. They downloaded the same information from their parents and from their parents before that. All this download comes down to you. Here you are, sitting in traffic, trying to make sales, and trying to have a great relationship. These things aren't working out. That's what you're cleaning on: the triggers that make you feel it's not working out. The more you clean and clear on those triggers, the more you remove the limitations and return to the natural state. It goes back to the Arnold Patent quote: "You don't create abundance. We create limitations." Clearing is getting rid of the limitations.

Some people will say, "Others need this. My teenagers need ho'oponopono to clean issues that they're dealing with."

When people learn this practice, they're often tempted to clean others or to tell others to clean themselves: "It's my husband who really needs this." Or the teenagers, the nasty coworkers, or the nasty boss.

Never tell someone else to clean themselves. Why?

Because everything is a mirror of what's in you. Those other people are mirrors of parts of you. If you try to wrestle with them, you're trying to change the mirror rather than changing yourself to improve your reflection in the mirror.

This is advanced material. I don't want to pull any punches here. I want you to realize that you have to take full responsibility. It is not about other people. Nobody else has to do ho'oponopono, ever. People still write to me and say, "I have this problem. Will you clean on it for me?" That's not ho'oponopono. Ho'oponopono is, you have this problem, and *you* clean on it. You take ownership of it.

Dr. Hew Len is retired now, but he used to receive emails from people saying, "Will you clean on this particular problem?" He would just say, "I'll clean." He meant that he was cleaning on his own life experience, but not necessarily on you, because you are in charge of your life experience.

One big mistake people make in ho'oponopono is to say, "OK, I've got it. I know I'm supposed to do cleaning, so let me go tell everybody else how to do it." If you'd really got it, you wouldn't tell anybody else. It's your job just to take care of you.

In the West, we think the way to influence people is to do some technique on them, or you have to have a great turn of phrase that is going to capture them. Once Gandhi was asked, "Please write down a message for me." He wrote down a reply: "I am my message."

Because of my background in marketing and copywriting, people would often ask, "How do you influence other people? How do you persuade other people? How do you manipulate other people?" I've studied NLP and various other persuasion techniques. I had different answers about what you would do. Today I understand that the only way to persuade, influence, or inspire anybody is through your own example. That's it. They're looking at you. They're watching. The kids are watching what the parents are doing. The parents can say all they like, but the kids are watching their behavior. You might say,

"Don't do this," but if they see you doing it, they're going to draw their own conclusions. Marcus Aurelius said, "Quit arguing about what a good man is. Be one."

Dr. Hew Len is living the example that he's teaching us. It's not about giving us phrases or slogans or T-shirts to lead us in some sort of parade. Maybe at some point it might happen through inspiration, but he's leading through example. That's the way to influence other people, if you want to influence them at all. Inspire them.

You can use this practice in business, like sales. One of the record-breaking car salespeople in the country is in California. He's a direct disciple of Dr. Hew Len. When I asked him, "How are you getting all your sales? What's your technique? How are you talking to people? How are you manipulating them? What's your NLP language advice?"

"I don't do any of that," he said. "I clean as I talk to them. They come up and say, 'My daughter's interested in a car.' I listen to whatever they're telling me. As they're talking to me, in my head, I'm saying, *I love you, I'm sorry, please forgive me, thank you. I love you, I'm sorry, please forgive me, thank you.*"

The salesman is carrying on a top-level conversation, but the subtext is ho'oponopono clearing. He says, "Without my trying, they buy cars. Often they come back and buy two or three. One time a guy came back and bought a car for everybody in his family." The salesman was laid-back, not a wolf of Wall Street, but more lamblike. In a subtle, ninjalike way, he was practicing ho'oponopono while conversing.

When Dr. Hew Len saw clients as a therapist, he didn't do ho'oponopono on any direct, audible level. He would talk to them: "What's your problem? What's going on? Why can't you sleep? Why can't you eat? Why are you losing weight? Why did you gain weight?" As he was listening to the problem, he was saying inside himself, *I love you, I'm sorry, please forgive me, thank you. I love you, I'm sorry, please forgive me, thank you.* He did cleaning and clearing on whatever was coming up. That's how he helped people therapeutically.

I've mentioned Mabel Katz, who is a ho'oponopono teacher. She was an IRS auditor. She would go into the offices and do the numbers game—"Show me your files and your tax returns"—but internally she was saying, *I love you, I'm sorry, please forgive me, thank you. I'm sorry, please forgive me, thank you.* She said she closed and freed more people from audits than any of the other agents. How do you account for this?

This is the easiest way to get results ever. While you're talking to people, inside, secretly, you're saying to yourself, *I love you, I'm sorry, please forgive me, thank you.* As you do it, miracles happen.

4

The Fifth Phrase

Up to now in all of my books on ho'oponopono I have only discussed the four core phrases: *I love you, I'm sorry, please forgive me, thank you.* Now I'm going to talk about the fifth phrase.

I learned from Dr. Hew Len that as you keep cleaning and clearing, you get closer and closer to Divinity, to zero, to the at-zero state. As you get closer to it, you start to receive inspiration. The inspiration is not coming from your memory, from your past, or your ego. It's coming from the Divine, by grace.

At one point I had set up a live advanced ho'oponopono certification weekend with Guitar Monk Mathew Dixon. It was outside of Austin. I was to speak two or three times over the weekend. As usual, I didn't really plan my talk. I didn't know what it would be about, although I knew it would be ho'oponopono-related. But I was practicing the four phrases, I was doing my meditation, I was having faith, I was trusting. I knew that when I got close to being on stage or was on stage, I would be visited by a message, so I was trusting that.

The night before I was to speak, I received the message in almost ghostly way, and it gave me the fifth phrases. I thought about the ones that came to me, and I thought they sounded awkward. I meditated on it, and I got the inspiration that it needed to be defined to be more useful.

I took it on faith. I took it as my marching orders. The next morning, when I got on stage, I said I would be delivering the fifth phrase. Everybody was quiet, on the edge of their seats. I wrote the fifth phrase down on a whiteboard and explained it. Everybody was moved, because they realized it was one of the most incredible cleaning and clearing statements ever.

A woman named Michelle Barr, who is an author and speaker in her own right, ran up afterwards with a big smile on her face. She said, "This fifth phrase is incredible. The fifth phrase means you no longer need to say the other four phrases."

I realized that she was right: the fifth phrase is so sweeping, so much more powerful that while you will still say the four phrases as you feel inspired, you don't need to, because the fifth phrase alone supersedes and transcends them.

The fifth phrase is, *I forgives myself.* This sounds like bad English. Why isn't it *I forgive myself*? Because that's not what we're actually saying.

I forgives myself. Let me explain this by breaking it down. First of all, the *I* is not referring to you; it is not about your personal self. When Dr. Hew Len was sending me emails, at the end he would write, "The peace of *I* be with you."

What was he referring to? *I* is referring to the *I* of God, the Great Something, the Great Mystery. It's referring to the whiteboard, the zero state. The *I* is the intelligence of the planet. Dr. Hew Len didn't mean the peace of himself; he meant the peace of *I.* The peace of *I* is the peace of the universe. May the peace of the universe be with you. Another way to state it is, the universe forgives my self. Dr. Hew Len always used the word *I* to refer to the universe or Divinity. *I forgives myself* is like saying *God forgives myself.*

Let's look at the other end: *myself. Myself* means the self that is the subconscious part of you, the child part of you, the part of you that is programmed and programmable. The part of you that has the limitations. If it were *Self* with a capital S, it would be referring to the superconscious, the higher consciousness part of you.

I forgives myself. The Divine forgives my programming, my limitations, my limited thinking, my—fill in the blank. *I forgives myself. Forgives* is there because we're talking about erasing what we've been holding on to. When we say, *I forgives myself,* it's basically saying that Grandpa God—whatever you want to call this figure—is not holding grudges against you. It's not holding a scorecard over you. It's not holding a prison journal entry of all your rights and wrongs in the eyes of the Divine. It's not doing that; you are. When you look at your life and you say, "The Divine forgives my transgressions; the Divine forgives my little self," then you, as the little self, can start to let go of guilt, grief, blame, remorse, or any of the heavy emotions that come from punishing yourself.

You can see that the fifth phrase has got nuclear depth to it, although it's not as simple as *I love you, I'm sorry, please forgive me, thank you.* Those phrases get you to this point, and they are still useful.

I mentioned earlier that I've gone through grief. My father passed away, my best friend passed away, a family member attempted suicide while I was going through a divorce. Grief has been a shadow in the background of my life. There were several nights that were dark nights of the soul, and I was walking the streets not wanting to live. And I was saying, *I love you, I'm sorry, please forgive me, thank you,* over and over.

What really helped me was saying the fifth phrase. I remember walking on these dark nights. The skies didn't even have stars, or if they were there, I wasn't seeing them because everything seemed bleak in my life. As I was walking, feeling the molasses of life weighing me down, I started repeating, *I forgives myself. I forgives myself.*

Then I started meditating on it. *I forgives myself.* What does that mean? It means, Joe, that the Divine forgives the little part of you that is feeling grief or remorse, that is feeling it's made a mistake. It's forgiving the little part of me, the ego part, that is hurting. It is saying, "Joe, you're off the hook. It is not your fault. It's your responsibility to feel well. It's your responsibility to do what the Divine orders or requests you to do. But you don't have to punish yourself, because the Divine is not punishing you. The Divine forgives myself. *I* forgives myself. The Great Something forgives my limited thinking."

That's the whole point of the fifth phrase, and that's the power of the fifth phrase. It's saying you're not being judged. You are actually being loved. I remember once when Dr. Hew Len came in from walking around in a garden. He had tears in his eyes, and he said, "The Divine just wants us to know that we are loved." I got chills. The Divine just wants you to know that you are loved. I really soak that up.

The Divine wants you to know that you are loved. The part of us that's not loving ourselves, that is judging ourselves is, again, the lowercase self. It's the ego system, the ecosystem of the subconscious mind. That's the part of us that's been programmed, that's programmable, that has all the limitations. That part of us looks at our lives and starts to judge us. But if it can allow the Divine to look at our lives, we go back to the Arnold Patent quote: "Abundance is our natural state. We create limitations. We create judgment. We create self-punishment." *I forgives myself* means freedom. It's like cutting the chains off.

We engage in many behaviors in life to feel loved, especially addictive behaviors—drugs, alcohol, sexual addictions. We want to feel loved by others physically, even though it might not lead to a feeling of genuine love. But if we break these down, it gets down to "I want to feel loved. I want to feel I'm acceptable." But the idea is that the Divine forgives.

If someone comes up to me and says, "Joe, I don't feel a need to clean anything in my life. What is it that I need to forgive? Things are going great for me. I'm not harboring ill will towards myself or anyone else." Does the fifth phrase even apply to that person?

I would say no. I'm in charge of my life; I'm not in charge of theirs. Dr. Hew Len once told me, "When you try to change other people, you're messing with their karma. And if you mess with their karma, you will have hell to pay." I don't know what the hell to pay would be, but in any case, I'm in charge of painting my life the way I want it to go. If somebody comes to me and asks me for advice, then maybe I could give it. But if somebody is strutting their stuff and feeling they're on top of the world, then Godspeed. Let them dance. Let them enjoy it.

This consideration does, however, lead to another: there are stages of consciousness in life. Even the ideas of *The Secret* and the law of attraction reflect a lower level of consciousness. It's better than victimhood, which is down at the bottom, but it's not the best. There's still one up. Ho'oponopono is more on the next level of consciousness.

People discover things like ho'oponopono when events don't go well. They have a death in the family, they have something traumatic happen; it could be a divorce or a lawsuit, an incurable illness for themselves or someone else. It could be any number of heavy things. They're walloped by this event; they're shaken. And when they're shaken, they look and ask, "What am I missing? What am I doing wrong? What do I need to do?" At that point, they might be open to ho'oponopono.

In many ways, somebody who doesn't think they have anything to clear on is at a level of innocence or ignorance, because we all have work to do. We all have our shortcomings, our programming, our limitations. But I don't want to interrupt anybody's parade. If they feel they're doing fantastically, let them keep going and enjoy.

One way of interpreting the fifth phrase is to say that the Great Something is forgiving your data. *Data*, again, is referring to our beliefs, stories, history, limitations—our baggage. The data in the computer is all of the things that weigh it down. If you have too much data, your computer won't work; it will be clogged up. If we have too much data in us around money, around lack and limitation, we won't have money. We will struggle with money, because the data will prevent us from having it. It's not that there isn't any money out there or that you don't deserve it; rather, the data will prevent you from attracting it and holding on to it. Data is any and all beliefs that are in the way of what you want to have, do, or be. Some belief systems serve you, and some don't. I want beliefs that serve me, or ultimately, as ho'oponopono teaches, I want to have no beliefs at all. You live from at-zero, from zero limits, from the whiteboard, and you get your marching orders from inspiration. The Divine forgives and is willing to erase everything else. We're the ones who typically hold on to it, our little selves thinking, "This is me. I was taught this way."

My father was born in 1925. By the time he was five, he was going through the Great Depression. The Great Depression programmed him in a strong way so that lack and limitation were tattooed on his brain. He lived to be ninety-three, but he never could let go of that conditioning; he didn't want to, because that's how he defined himself, but the Great Something would have just let it go. He could have gotten to the point where he thought, "You know what? I should let that go. I'm ninety-three. I should buy a car or something."

It isn't the Divine that's stopping you from having what you want, from healing, from having more sales or more business. It's our little selves. It's our data. The Great Something forgives our data. Reflect on that, and you can lighten your load and move to at-zero.

One of the basic principles of ho'oponopono is taking full responsibility. You say, "I don't have as much money as I want right now." If you come from full responsibility, you have to say, "I've got something to do with that fact. There must be some beliefs, some limitations in me. Some paradigm of lack and limitation is preventing money from coming to me. Because I'm taking full responsibility, I've got to own that."

What do we do about it? In ho'oponopono, *I forgives myself* means that the Divine forgives my thoughts about money, my belief in lack and limitation, and my self-constructed mental paradigms about receiving cash.

Abundance is your state of being, but limitations are created by you. If you want to remove those limitations, *I* forgives them. The Great Something forgives my lack and limitation; the great God of the universe releases, erases, forgives, and removes any and all thoughts around money. In this case, *I forgives myself* means that *I* is working on the parts of you that feel lack and limitation concerning money.

Money doesn't have any beliefs about you; you have beliefs about it. Remove these beliefs, and money is waiting; it's circulating all around. It's waiting for somebody to appreciate it, which brings it into your life. When you don't appreciate it, you're not seeing it. You still think money is the root of all evil, which is not true. You want to clean on, clear on, remove, and delete those beliefs. *I forgives my limitation. The Divine forgives my limited thinking.* All these are variations on one theme: let's make peace with money.

Let me talk a little now about how to use this phrase, or the other phrases. When you want to use ho'oponopono on some issue, you hold it in your mind, your awareness, your body, your physical system. You might visualize it or feel it emotionally, but you want to be conscious of it in some way. As you're holding it in your mind, you can say, *I forgive my self* or *I love you, I'm sorry, please forgive me, thank you.*

I find that ho'oponopono works dramatically better when you are holding the issue in your mind and feeling it. You're not just talking about it, like, "I've got a problem with so-and-so." No, feel it as if you're going to go to a bar later and drink yourself silly, because this is really bothering you. I'm not advocating that, but I am saying that when you feel it, feel it deeply and rawly. You're holding it in your awareness, you're holding it in your consciousness, and it's up for healing at that point. That's when you can say *I love you, I'm sorry, please forgive me, thank you* or *I forgives myself.*

You may ask if other ho'oponopono phrases will come in the future. All I can do is speculate on that. I think there will be other phrases, other cleaning tools, other things that come to different people through inspiration. For example, I've made a number of instrumental albums with Guitar Monk Mathew Dixon; we do a lot of ho'oponopono things together. He is my guitar teacher and my partner on some albums. One day I'd gotten this brand-new guitar made by Linda Manzer in Toronto, who's a very well-known luthier. Mathew looked at it and he said, "It's a cleaning tool." And I looked and I thought, "He's right." I picked it up, started playing it, and I felt I was being healed. I was being cleansed and cleared by this acoustic guitar made by Linda Manzer. Was it a clearing tool? We both agreed that it was, because in that moment, through inspiration, we felt that it was.

I know one time I showed Dr. Hew Len my new business card. At that time I had a car, a 2005 Panoz, which I called Francine. It was on my card. I gave it to Dr. Hew Len. He smiled and said, "This is a clearing tool."

"The business card?"

"Yes. You could use this. When you think of a problem, imagine cutting it up." In other words, I visualize the problem, and I imagine taking the card and slicing it with scissors.

There will be other cleaning and clearing tools, but can we all agree on what's clearing and what isn't? I don't think so. Somebody else could look at the guitar and say, "It's just a guitar." Somebody else could look at my business card and say, "Give me a break. It's your business card. It's not cleaning anything." It's in the eye of the beholder.

I've been asked why the fifth phrase was revealed. It came by grace. *Grace* is a funny word, but that's how the Divine works. We can beg, plead, pray, stomp our feet, yell at the sky, and tell God to do such and such, but what comes to you comes by grace. Grace has a certain magic to it, and you can't make it happen. If you do, that's the ego. If grace is really coming as a gift from the Divine, it comes when the Divine is ready to deliver the gift. I was open, I made time to receive, and lo and behold, I received.

5

High-Level Ho'oponopono

Advancing to the Fourth Stage of Awakening

In this book, we've been covering ho'oponopono at a much deeper and advanced level than I've ever done for the general public before. Now I'd like to talk about the four stages of awakening and show how a regular practice of this process can help one to advance to the higher stages. The practice of ho'oponopono, and the fifth phrase in particular, can do more than help a person with a problem or situation: it can lead to a transformed, more joyful way of living.

We've talked about clearing and cleaning, but how did this debris accumulate in our consciousness to begin with? Dr. Hew Len says we have inherited programming all the way from the beginning of time. Depending on what mood he's in, he will also say we've downloaded information from outer space and aliens. Whatever way you look at it, we've received a lot of garbage. Certain things may have been useful for survival at one time, but they're still with us, inhibiting us and keeping us in a state of limitation.

Sometimes I ask people, "Were your parents Mr. and Mrs. Buddha?" People will laugh and say, "No." So your parents had limiting beliefs, most of which you downloaded innocently from them. Nobody tried to wire you, but they had lack and limitation programmed into them. So did their parents. We can trace this centuries back to the beginning of time. Cavemen and cavewomen probably starved a great deal and were in fear for their lives, so they no doubt believed we live in a universe that was scary and full of scarcity, because in that period, it probably was.

When you get down to the present moment in history, you have so much programming, so much unconscious wiring, that you have no clue where it came from. Yet there it is, and you're operating from it unconsciously. It becomes pretty overwhelming.

Where did it start? I don't really know. Do we have it? Absolutely. You do, I do, we all do. What we're here to do is awaken from it. We're here to remove those limitations, to clean and clear the garbage that keeps us away from Divinity so that we can be Divinity living itself through us. We can receive inspirations that help us lead more glorious lives.

At this point, let me go through the four stages of awareness. Stage one is *victimhood*. Some have even argued that victimhood is not a stage of awakening, because you are pretty much unconscious. You're thinking that you're a victim, so it's tough to say that that's really a stage of awakening. Nevertheless, it's a stage of consciousness we need to look at.

As Thoreau said, "Most people lead lives of quiet desperation." That's the victimhood mentality. Victimhood is blaming everybody else, because for you, it's everybody else's fault. You have next to nothing to do with what happens to you, because you're a victim. Most people live their lives as victims and go to their deaths feeling like victims. Most of history is about victim consciousness.

If somebody is lucky, they see a movie like *The Secret*. They read a book, maybe this one. They can exit victimhood and move into the next stage, which is *empowerment*.

Empowerment is thrilling. It's when you grow wings. It's when you begin to feel as if you're Superman or Superwoman and virtually anything is possible. In many cases, that's true. Virtually anything is.

Empowerment is completely different from victimhood. With victimhood, you have no power. With empowerment, you're starting to feel your oats. You're starting to feel, "Man, I can command things to happen, and they will happen."

This is a wonderful stage to be at—certainly it beats victimhood—but it's not the final stage. As I've already mentioned, at some point one reaches a crisis. It could be a death: a parent or loved one dies. Either you or someone close to you has to deal with an illness; it could be an accident, it could be anything that somebody considers big and hairy; it's something they can't handle by themselves.

That's when people start to move into the third stage, which I call *surrender*. There are two kinds of surrender. There's the surrender when you give up and you say, "I can't win. I'm just dead." That brings you back to victimhood. That's not the surrender I mean; that's giving up.

The kind of surrender I'm talking about is giving in to your internal connection to the Divine. It's where something like ho'oponopono is perfect, because it brings you back into your connection to the whiteboard, to zero, to inspiration. You're surrendering not like a victim, but in an empowered way. It's almost like enlightened empowerment. Surrender is the stage where you join forces with the Divine. It isn't you against the world: now you and the Divine are cocreators in the world.

That's the third stage. There's still a fourth. This one only comes by grace. There's no way to make it happen.

You can't leverage yourself into it. You can't earn enough points to get it. It comes by the grace of the universe by the grace of the Divine itself.

The fourth stage is what I call *awakening*. Awakening is enlightenment. It is where the Divine lives and breathes through you. You, as an entity, no longer feel separate.

At the beginning of this book, I said that what is really dividing everybody is the belief that we're separate from the Divine. That's the first division. It creates all the other divisions, because now we feel we're alone in the universe, isolated from everything.

The stage of awakening reunites us. That's when the Divine and you are one. It's when the Divine lives, thinks, acts, breathes, and lives through your body, mind, soul, and spirit. It only comes from grace, because your ego has to be out of the way for it to happen. If your ego says, "I know how to become enlightened," no, because your ego wouldn't be there. Your ego would never even say that. That is not possible.

The exit strategy for awakening is to prepare for it. Ho'oponopono is a wonderful way to do that. You're deleting all your limiting programs; you're moving back into forgiveness, into a space of love and gratitude; you're making time for meditation and gratitude. These are all wonderful means of paving the way for an awakening, but the awakening comes by grace.

———————

Let's go through the four stages in more detail.

I would say the vast majority of people are born into stage one and stay there. We don't come into life as a blank slate. Ho'oponopono philosophy and psychology, and the ancient cultural customs, teach that you come in with traits that you're preprogrammed to have because of limitations inherited from your family. The science of epigenetics says that what your great grandparents may have had in their bodies may have skipped a generation or two and may show up in your body. That doesn't mean you're destined to have these traits and you can't change them. It does mean that when you're born, you don't come in as a blank slate.

Once I had a litter of nine cats. They all came from the same father and the same mother, but every single one had a different personality. How was that possible? They had to come in with some sort of programming. They had to come in with some sort of wiring that took place before I ever got there.

We're the same way. When we're born, we are given life, but it's given in a vessel that already has some programming. Most of that program is not abundance-oriented. It comes from what people went through beforehand, which was lack, scarcity, and survival: "How do I get my next meal?" "How do I get security?" "How do I get a loved one so I can keep my lifeline going?"

When we're born, we're downloading information from people who were not Mr. and Mrs. Buddha; they were Mr. and Mrs. Limitations. They had their own baggage. They didn't know it, any more than anybody else before them knew it. Working on yourself was not as popular then as it is today. Today it's more of an in thing to do self-work. Back then, not so much so.

It's easy to see why people would be victims. They come in programmed for lack, limitation, and scarcity, and they think the world's against them from the moment of birth. Then they're raised by parents who instill in them the ideas of survival and how to make it in the world, but empowerment—that's very rare.

Telltale signs of the first stage? You blame other people. If you say anybody else is responsible, you are raising your hand and saying, "I am a victim." I don't care if you say it's the president, the economy, the political system, your neighbor. That's your telltale sign right there.

You want to leave victimhood. If you're reading this book, you probably either have or are in the process of doing so. It's highly unlikely that a victim would invest in this book unless they'd already moved the needle a little bit towards empowerment.

Now we're in empowerment. How do you know you're in empowerment? You're starting to state intentions; you're starting to take actions; you're starting to set goals; you're starting to engage in more positive habits every day; you're starting to use more positive psychology; you're thinking good things about yourself and other people. You're stretching, you're learning, you're growing. You're doing things that you never would have thought of doing as a victim, because you didn't think it was possible or that you deserved it. Now that you're in the empowerment stage, it's, "Bring it on. Whatever it is, let's do it, because it's possible. Let's go for it."

Most people who teach traditional success techniques are probably at the empowerment level. You'll find Tony Robbins here, even though he is a big fan of ho'oponopono and has been teaching it onstage.

When I studied with singer Melissa Etheridge and had a songwriting workshop at her house, I gave her copies of *At Zero* and *Zero Limits*. She already knew about it. She said Tony Robbins taught her and a few other people about ho'oponopono. Here you have one of the big success gurus, who does talk about goal setting and empowerment. He's very much an empowerment cheerleader, but he's also learning about ho'oponopono.

The Zig Ziglars and Dale Carnegies of the world are going to be more in empowerment. Napoleon Hill has some writings that lead into surrender. If you look at *The Master Laws of Success*, for example, some of that work hints that he understood these principles, although he didn't know what ho'oponopono was.

Empowerment is wonderful; I am not dismissing it. I still use that material today. It's fortifying, growth-oriented material. It's empowering, which is exactly why it's in the empowerment stage. You know you're in that stage when you're doing things for yourself and others, and you're setting goals, and you're working the system.

Then, of course, you want to move into surrender. A lot of people get into surrender because they bumped up against something they couldn't handle by themselves. This is where you think, "I thought I was in control of my life, but my dad or my mom was dying, and I couldn't stop it. I thought I was in control of my life, but if I were, they'd still be alive."

Something else was in charge. Because of that, people start searching and reaching, and they become more open. That's when they discover books that will take them in the direction of working on the inside of themselves. They'll begin the search, not only to find meaning but to find a connection to Source. They'll use different words: "I want a connection to God." "I want a connection to the universe." "I want a connection to Spirit."

Whatever it happens to be, they've surrendered to a higher power. It, too, is a wonderful place to be. It's even better than empowerment, because you actually have more power. In empowerment, you're still you against the universe. With surrender, it's you *with* the universe. Big difference.

How do you know you're in surrender? Basically, you're surrendering. You may be praying more. I wrote a book called *The Secret Prayer*, in which I said most prayers should begin with gratitude. Instead of beginning with begging—"give me, give me, give me"—it's beginning with thank you. Thank you for what I've got. Thank you for my life. You spend more time in prayer; you spend more time meditating; you spend more time in gratitude; you spend more time doing the four phrases or the fifth phrase; you spend more time in the silence.

I wrote a book on P. T. Barnum, the great circus promoter, called *There's a Customer Born Every Minute*. I really researched the man. I wanted to understand how he became such a great success as a marketer, a politician, a writer, a speaker, and an entrepreneur.

I went to Barnum's grave in Bridgeport, Connecticut. You'd think there would be a giant statue, but there was a tiny marker on his gravestone from 1891. It contains his motto, which he said is what he carried through his entire life. He went through the death of his wife. He had two fires in his museum. He went through bankruptcy. He went through some dark nights. It was not all circus time for this guy. He lived to be eighty years old. What's on that marker? "Not my will, but thine be done. —P. T. Barnum."

Most people think Barnum said things like, "There's a sucker born every minute," but he never said that. He actually came from a very respectful, internally connected perspective. Of course, he didn't know anything about ho'oponopono, but this attitude—"Not my will, but thine be done"—is the essence of the surrender state. It worked for P. T. Barnum.

You may ask whether the regular practice of ho'oponopono helps people advance to stage four. You can and should control the process of going from stage one to stage two, because you're moving from victimhood to empowerment. There's some control in terms of taking charge and taking responsibility for your life and so forth. Can you do it the same with going from three to four?

Going from stage three to stage four is not like that, because it's where you have to let go. Wanting to control it is the opposite of letting go. You have to totally surrender, which is the stage itself.

"Not my will, but thine be done" is actually a clearing statement. The more I sit with it, it more it sounds like ho'oponopono. "Not my will": that means get out of my ego, get out of the limitations, the small me, the little self. "Not my will but thine" means that there is a higher power—the Great Something, the Great Mystery, Gaia. That's the will that is being done through me. I love that as a statement to meditate on: "Not my will, but thine be done."

Stage three is not about stopping or quitting life. You don't get to go sit in a corner and do nothing. You still have whatever your mission is. P. T. Barnum's mission was to be a circus and museum promoter, author, and speaker.

For the longest time, the Divine wanted Dr. Hew Len to do seminars. At one point, he called me and he said, "The Divine says you have to write the book *Zero Limits*."

You don't stop living; you don't stop doing things. What's different? First, you pay more attention to your inspiration: what the Divine is saying is your calling or your marching orders. Whatever those are, you go and follow them.

Second, you follow your orders with trust, knowing that you're doing your part in the game of life. You're contributing your piece of the puzzle. You do it in a relaxed way, knowing that this is important and we need you to play your part in it.

You let go of how the results come out because you're not caught up in them. In many ways, you know that there really is no end result. Life just keeps unfolding. There's another minute, and another minute, and another minute; it just keeps going. In my case, you write over seventy books. You stop, look back, and ask, "I did that?" You're doing it because in each moment, you follow what the moment is asking you to do, and you do it with trust and knowingness.

I've already told about the IRS auditor doing ho'oponopono and the salesman making records selling cars. He's still selling cars even while he's in stage three, surrender. Surrender doesn't mean stop. Surrender doesn't mean give up. Surrender doesn't mean pull over, you're not going anywhere anymore. In many ways, you may become more active and do more things, but you'll do them with a joyous, happy, trusting quality. That will make a dramatic difference in your life, your well-being, your health, and your happiness. Werner Erhard, who did the EST seminars way back in the seventies, said, "If God told you what to do, you'd do it, and you'd be happy." Well, you're doing what God wants you to do.

When I was in the Ukraine, a woman with a very popular television show said, "You say everybody should be doing what they love."

"Yes."

"Well, if we all do what we love, who's going to clean up the garbage? Who's going to do the plumbing?"

"You are assuming there aren't garbage people who are happy. There are plumbers who are happy."

When I was in Chicago years ago, the plumbing in the hotel needed work. A plumber came up, and he was the happiest plumber I'd ever seen in my life. He was happy to do his job. He was clear-headed, with a big smile on his face.

That's what happens. You end up playing your part, whether you're the garbage pickup person or the traffic control person or the plumber or the author or the interviewer. You do your part. It doesn't mean you cure cancer.

If it ends up being that, Godspeed to you, go do it, but it could just be raising your kids.

The Bible says, "If you have faith the size of a mustard seed, anything shall be possible." I love talking about the mustard seed. I actually carry a mustard seed coin that has this verse engraved around it, with an actual mustard seed in the center. Sometimes I'll do a magic trick and have it appear in somebody's hand, and then explain to them that you have to have faith.

Once I was onstage at a speaking event, and I told the mustard seed story. I held up the seed. I said, "A mustard seed doesn't have any doubts. It's going to grow up to be a mustard tree. It's going to grow up to expand from what it already is. It's not going to become a rose. It's not going to become a loaf of bread. It's not going to turn into something or somebody else. It's got no doubts: 'This is who I am. This is what I'm going to be, and I am on track to do it.'

"Well," I said, "what if you had no doubts? What if you came from that faith?"

Part of the problem that we have in practicing ho'oponopono is wimpy faith. We don't really believe that we're connected. We don't really believe anything is on our side. We don't really believe that we're taking care of our lack and limitation. As a result, we don't really try; we don't go for anything. We're practicing a wimpy faith. If we take on the whole meaning of the mustard seed parable, we can achieve the impossible and perform miracles, like Jesus. If we really take that on, we could be inspired at new energy levels that we can't even imagine right now.

Many of us get caught up in our own doubts: "I doubt that this is working. I doubt that ho'oponopono actually works for me. I doubt that the four phrases or the fifth phrase are clearing tools."

You can doubt all over the place and not achieve anything because you are doubting. Dr. Hew Len would say that's all nonsense. It's all coming from the mind, and your mind is going to come up with all kinds of riddles, stories, questions, fears, doubts. I created a photo on Instagram with the caption, "Doubt your doubts and go for your dreams." When you doubt your doubts, you start to move in the direction of the fourth stage.

If you're sitting in the third or second stage, and you're saying to yourself, "I doubt that I'll ever get it," you won't be able even to approach the concept. Your doubt is preventing you from even stepping up to the window to look in. Doubt your doubts: do your best to remove them so you're back into the moment with gratitude and clarity.

Next comes one of the most important things in this book. It's an exercise we need to do on a moment-by-moment basis: realize that even as you're reading, there is a background whiteboard to your consciousness. It's consciousness itself. The more you can identify with that background whiteboard, the closer you will be to awakening. The more you can see past appearances to the Source, to the witness, to the essence that is the background, the more you will step into awakening.

This is a profound thing that I'm trying to describe. I can understand that it's confusing, so I'm going to try one more time. When I speak, I'm aware of my speaking. I'm also aware that this is like a movie: there's a screen upon which everything I'm saying and doing is being projected. The more I can identify with that screen and go back to the whiteboard, the more I can see that everything I'm saying is being projected onto it. The more I can see this process, the closer I am to awakening.

The awakening is my merging with the whiteboard. Once you are awakened, you'll still have words, you'll still speak. All the enlightened masters, with a few exceptions, still spoke. They may not have written anything—most of them did not—but they did speak. They still had things to say because inspiration was coming through them. At that point of awakening, you're like a ventriloquist's puppet: the Divine is pulling the strings, feeding you the lines, and having you look this way and that; it's living through you.

I know this is complicated and confusing because this is not a state of human nature that everybody has in common. There are over seven billion people on the planet. One or two might be enlightened. The rest of us are bumbling around, trying to make it work, and the vast majority of them, as Thoreau said, are in victimhood, leading lives of quiet desperation.

Let me emphasize again that even at the fourth stage, there's still nothing wrong with living in the material world and enjoying things here. The material and spiritual are two sides of the same coin. You look at one side and say it's material, but you look on the other side or inside, and there's the spiritual. You may still want a wonderful car or a wonderful home, or you still may want to contribute to a cause you believe in. It'll still be unique to you, and you will still participate in the world and the games of the world. You'll do it with an elevated state of awareness. That's the difference. In fact, you'll do it practicing the presence of God. From a ho'oponopono standpoint, you'll see the Divine in everything. You'll see the Divine in this book, on the wall, in flowers, in water, whatever you look. It's practicing the presence of the Divine.

Personally I would prefer to avoid the idea of going into the fourth stage of awakening as a goal, because that's counter to what you actually want. You want to let go so that you're given this awakening by grace.

I do daily meditation or ho'oponopono not only to prepare myself for the fourth stage, but also for the benefits that I get now. My father worked out every day for over seventy years. I don't think he ever missed a day. In fact, he died in the gym; that's how important it was to him. He said that he wasn't working out to live longer; he was working out for today. He said, "I work out because I feel better today."

A lot of people have this kind of motivation: "If I do this, I will extend my life, or I will get some result way down the road." My father was of the frame of mind that if I do this today, I get a result today. I think we should practice ho'oponopono, meditation, and gratitude with the same mindset. I'm doing the cleaning and clearing today, for today. If, by grace that leads to an awakening, thank you, God. But I am doing the cleaning and clearing so I am better, I am serene, I am tranquil, I am evolving now. I am exceeding my own personal best. I'm doing it for today; I'm doing it for now.

6

The X Phrase

Developing Your Own Phrases for Greater Spiritual Growth

Suppose that people have worked with the first five phrases for some time. It's become a regular part of the running dialogue in their heads. At this point they may want to tap into increased levels of healing and spiritual awakening pertaining to more personal situations. We can then ask whether there are other phrases that are out there to be discovered.

Dr. Hew Len told me that as you keep cleaning, you will receive inspiration. In other words, you may start with *I love you, I'm sorry, please forgive me, thank you.* Then as you progress, as you keep using those phrases, you may be inspired to eliminate a couple of them, as I've mentioned. You may end up with *thank you,* or *I love you,* or you may receive a new phrase that's unique to you and your situation. As we keep doing the cleaning and the clearing, we're dispelling the clouds from our awareness so that we can receive inspiration.

As I've already emphasized, in every moment, you're coming from either memory or inspiration. Most of the time, we're coming from memory. As we keep doing ho'oponopono, we're erasing more and more of that memory so we can receive inspiration.

Some of this inspiration can consist of words or phrases. Let me give you an example. Decades ago, I came across the word *benestrophe.* Whenever I used it, people would say, "Is that Latin? What are you saying? What is that word? What does it mean?" *Benestrophe,* as I remember, was a word coined by Marilyn Ferguson, author of *The Aquarian Conspiracy,* back in the seventies. It was meant to be the opposite of *catastrophe.* A catastrophe is when a whole lot of things go bad all at once. *Benestrophe* is the opposite: it's when a whole lot of wonderful things happen all at once. I thought, "Oh, I want benestrophes. I want to live a benestrophe kind of life." Very often in business I'll say, "I'm looking for a benestrophic outcome; I'm looking for a benestrophe."

For me, *benestrophe* is a clearing tool. It is a new word that I use to clear. I don't go around saying it to people, any more than I go around saying, *I love you, I'm sorry, please forgive me, thank you* aloud. It's my internal experience. When I say *benestrophe* silently, it is as a new, modernized ho'oponopono word that I use to help me get clear.

Let me give you another example. The life partner I'm with today is Lisa Winston. Lisa is a best-selling author, she's got her own TV show, but she's been fighting Lyme disease. She's using ho'oponopono to help herself get clear and heal. As she's doing it, she came up with the phrase, *Be brave enough*. When I heard it and felt it, I thought, "This is a powerful phrase," because in the self-help movement, they say things like, "Just do it," "Be strong," and "Be fearless." There's a whole lot of rah-rah, but people who are suffering with something that feels incurable can't muster up the strength to believe in it. *Be brave enough* implies that you don't have to be the bravest, you don't have to be the strongest; you just have to be brave enough for today.

This becomes an empowering new clearing tool. It may not make sense to a lot of other people unless they need to believe in themselves. Maybe they can start saying, "Be brave enough. Just be brave enough. Just be brave enough for today." In fact, we're writing a song called "Be Brave Enough," because we want to get that message out.

As we keep using ho'oponopono, wherever we come in, we grab the tail that says, *I love you, I'm sorry, please forgive me, thank you*. Maybe we get more advanced and we start doing *I forgives myself.* At some point, there will be an awakening and a clarity so that you can receive an inspiration for something unique to you. When it comes and you know that it is right for you, own it, use it, and share it, much as I've been doing here.

Some people will ask if there's a period of time during which beginners should be using the core phrases before they start developing their own phrases. This question suggests that there are rules, regulations, and finer points that ho'oponopono doesn't really have. It's basically an inside job. I don't want to say somebody has to be doing things for a certain period of time before they can allow new inspiration to come. Since inspiration is coming from the Divine and it comes by grace, why can't it come the very first day, the very first time somebody says, *I love you, I'm sorry, please forgive me, thank you*? It's entirely possible, so I don't want to be the guy putting up roadblocks, saying, "No, no. It's too soon for inspiration for you. You need to do it for two years."

This is all an inside job. It's a very much subjective experience. It's very much a spiritual connection: your connection to your divinity. For me to step into your internal world seems like a violation, at least for my mindset. It's far more respectful to say, "Treat this as a meditation. It's between you and your connection to this higher power that's giving us life and animating our being." That unique relationship will guide you.

These phrases—*I love you, I'm sorry, please forgive me, thank you*—are like little rudders on an airplane. We're using them to move through life. As we do, we could be inspired, because the clouds are parting.

Dr. Hew Len would call me Joseph all the time rather than just Joe. At one point, he said he was receiving inspiration to give me a Hawaiian name. I thought, "That's cool. I wonder what my Hawaiian name would be." We're all curious about these things. He said, "It's Ao Akua." First, I had to ask him how to pronounce it. Second, what does it mean? *Ao Akua* means the *parting of the clouds to see God*. That sounds pretty cool. *Ao Akua* has become a cleaning tool for me. It may not be for somebody else, because they may not resonate with it. Again, they have to check inside.

My whole point is, as you do ho'oponopono, you are in effect doing Ao Akua. You are parting the clouds to see God. As you part the clouds—the clouds being the memories, doubts, fears, limitations, the mental programming that obstruct the miracle of this moment—you see what's behind the clouds. We'll say it's the sky, but *sky* is like a code word for the Divine. That's the witness. That witness, that Divinity, that sky can whisper a new word, a new phrase, even a new symbol to you.

Ho'oponopono believes not only that everything is alive, but that everything has a purpose. Everything nurtures you in some way. Eating strawberries or blueberries is a cleaning tool. According to Dr. Hew Len, when some-body was sick and went to Morrnah, who was considered to be a kahuna and a healer, for help, she would go in the garden, where she had many herbs and plants. There she would ask, "Who wants to help this woman heal?" Then she would look for the plants that raised their hands, so to speak. She'd pull those plants to make a herbal tea or concoction to give to the person that was ill. The whole point is that everything is alive, which means anything could be a cleaning tool.

I've talked various cleaning tools: a guitar by Linda Manzer, my business card with my Panoz car on it, words like *benestrophe*. Dr. Hew Len and Morrnah talked about plants and fruits. This opens up the planet or the galaxy, depending on how far you want to stretch your mind.

Dr. Hew Len said that blue solar water is a cleaning tool. Blue solar water is simply water that you get any-where; it can be tap water. You put it in a blue glass bottle, and you set it in the sun, usually for a day, but it could be for an hour or so. The sun is doing its magic to that water through the blue-tinted bottle. Then you bring the water in and you drink it.

The list goes on. I could jokingly say that carrot cake is a cleaning tool, but I would be forcing it. I really like carrot cake, so if I said it's a clearing tool, I could get away with eating more of it and get away with it. I could try to make it a cleaning tool, although inside myself, I know it isn't. It doesn't feel as if it is. If it came from inspiration at some point, maybe it could be.

The point is that because of that discernment within myself, I know when something is a clearing tool and when it isn't. When you feel something is a clearing tool, ask yourself, "Is it really coming from inspiration, or do I want this to be a clearing tool for some hidden agenda?"

All of this is just to say, keep practicing ho'oponopono. You will part the clouds to see God.

A lot of questions may come up: Are there elements of a well-constructed ho'oponopono phrase? Is short better? Should it be in the present tense or future-oriented? Oriented toward oneself or others? What elements might be helpful for people who are looking to develop a phrase?

The most helpful thing to do is throw out the rulebook. In the self-help industry, there's a lot of talk about how to word an affirmation and how to structure a goal. They talk about using the present tense and the first person. All of that makes sense in the second stage of empowerment. Here you're trying to set goals or create scripts or affirmations that will empower you to get the results you want. From the second stage of empowerment, that is priceless. It's useful information that we should all know and implement.

For the higher stages, we don't want any of that. Look at the fifth phrase: *I forgives myself.* It's bad English; it violates the rules of grammar. It's initially confusing. Is it three words (*I forgives myself*) or four (*I forgives my self*)? Actually, it's three words.

Then it gets even more complicated. When you translate these phrases into other languages, you go into the meanings of the words, because their equivalents of *to forgive* could have subtle differences depending on the language you're in. When I went to countries like Russia, Ukraine, Poland, and Italy, a common statement that I heard was, "The four phrases mean something different in our language."

If we really try to structure a phrase that's going to appease everybody including our English teacher, we will fail. We have to honor the inspiration when it comes. The night the fifth phrase came to me, I resisted it. I was thinking, "Wait a minute. I'm an author. I'm a writer. I can't put out something that says *I forgives*. It doesn't make any sense. It's not grammatically correct." I had to go within myself and use discernment. This is something we all need to learn—the discernment to know the difference. Is it coming from my intellect, or is it coming from my inspiration? Is it coming from my brain, my mind, or is it coming from my gut, my feelings?

People often ask how you know the difference between intuition and intellect (which is similar to the difference between memory and inspiration). Most of the time, memory and intellect are head-oriented. We all know the feeling of thinking. It seems to take place in our skull, behind our eyes. It feels as if the computer's running right up between my ears. That's also where memory seems to be.

Intuition and inspiration come more from the body. In Japanese and Hawaiian culture, they talk about the point around your navel area. Some spiritual beliefs say your seed of consciousness is not in your head; it's in your belly.

Use this criterion as a way to detect where the signal is coming from. When the fifth phrase came to me, I had to look within myself and discern: is it coming from the neck up or from the neck down? It really felt as if it was coming from below; I felt I was receiving it rather than making it. As an author and copywriter, I know what it's like to structure copy, write sentences, and word things in such a way as to get the greatest impact. I was not doing that with the fifth phrase. It came from the sky—from the whiteboard, from the world, from God.

I received the fifth phrase within and checked within myself: it came from the felt, bodily sense. If there's any rule for structuring these phrases or images, it's that when you receive them, check within yourself, because self-deception and self-sabotage are rampant. We are for the most part unconscious of our own behavior. We want to check within ourselves. Is it coming from the head or the heart? We want to come from the heart.

Receiving the phrase could come from the outside. For example, you could be reading this book, and there could be a word or phrase that seems to light up for you. It'll be lighting up for you personally, not for me. I probably didn't highlight it in the book, but as you're reading, there may be something here that clicks for you. That's the kind of thing you want to pay attention to.

As people practice ho'oponopono, they may receive an inspiration for a word, a phrase, a symbol, or an object, or they may read a book or watch a movie and have something click in them. It'll feel like, "Oh. That movie, that book, that line, that person, that character, that color, that coat even—that scarf is a clearing tool." The inspiration will be unique to them. They won't make it happen. They won't structurally, logically, try to control it; they'll more or less receive it by grace.

7

Advanced Cleaning Methods

In this chapter, we're going to go into other cleaning methods in the ho'oponopono philosophy. As I've been saying, ho'oponopono is more than a series of phrases. It is a spiritual way of being; in many ways, it's a new paradigm for your life.

Some people may have anxieties about destructive imitations of cleaning methods. Somebody might unconsciously sabotage themselves by saying, "Cocaine is a cleaning tool." When they take cocaine, they feel good. This might reinforce the idea that it's a great clearing tool: "I feel better now, so I want more cocaine."

Let's interrupt that thought, because we're looking for things that bring us health and happiness. Ho'opono-pono teaches that strawberries are a tool for healing and cleansing, but I don't think anybody would say strawberries are bad for you. Maybe if you had an allergic reaction to it, you wouldn't eat strawberries. You could eat something else that is considered to be a cleaning tool.

In one of the early ho'oponopono events that I attended with Dr. Hew Len, there was a bowl of M&M's. At that point I was in a fitness contest. I felt M&M's were the devil; I didn't want to be anywhere near them. Then Dr. Hew Len announced that M&M's were a clearing tool.

I went to Dr. Hew Len and said, "How can M&M's be a clearing or cleansing tool? They're sugar, they're chocolate, they're addictive. They're not good for you, and I am in a fitness contest, so keep this away from me."

"You don't have to eat one," he said. "You can just lick it." I was thinking, "Who would lick an M&M and put it back? This is getting even more cruel."

All of this goes back to a sense of discernment. What is good for you? M&M's were not good for me, especially during the fitness phase that I was going through. I would not say M&M's were a cleaning tool for me at that period in time.

That's the first level. There's the subjective experience of "Is this really good for me?" Then we have to look at whether we are deceiving ourselves: "Hey, let's do some cocaine. It's really a clearing tool, wink, wink, and we'll do more of it." We all know and agree that cocaine is not a cleaning or clearing tool. It is not good for you or anybody else. We want to look at everything from a blunt tough-love viewpoint: this is not good for us, so let's stay away from it.

This is why we want to keep doing ho'oponopono. We're easily deceived by ourselves. Research in neuroscience and neuropsychology says we are unconsciously driven in almost every moment. This is exactly what ho'oponopono says: we come from memory or we come from inspiration. What is memory? It is the unconscious database of past experiences, stories, and beliefs that have filled our brains in order to get us to here. We still live out of those projections. We still live out of the unconscious mind. We want to clean it up. How? We begin with *I'm sorry, please forgive me, thank you, I love you, I forgives myself*, then perhaps *benestrophe* or whatever else comes up next. As we keep cleaning, we'll have greater clarity about the cleaning tool that is happy, helpful, and best for us.

The first thing I want to say to anybody going through addictions is to be easy on yourself. It's tempting to beat yourself up because you're doing something that you don't really want to do, although you are unconsciously driven to keep doing it. Be easy on yourself, love yourself, nurture yourself, care for yourself. You're not alone: a lot of people have the same addiction. Love yourself; appreciate yourself.

Dr. Hew Len said, "As you do ho'oponopono on an issue, for example on addiction, you will be inspired to find something that will help you." As you're saying *I love you, I'm sorry, please forgive me, thank you* or *I forgives myself* or any other ho'oponopono phrases, you will be led to a book, a seminar, a therapist, a person, or some other way of breaking the habit. Don't think that ho'oponopono is the only thing to do. It could clean and clear the way for an inspiration about the next thing to do.

It's real easy to sit there and saying, "I've been doing ho'oponopono for twenty-four hours, but I'm still overeating or smoking," As you're doing ho'oponopono, maybe you received an inspiration, for example, to look into hypnotherapists in your area to handle that particular addiction. Whatever the inspiration is, act on it.

Inspired action is extremely important. With ho'oponopono, you don't just sit on the beach and stop living. As you practice, you will be receiving inspiration, and you'll live your life doing what is unique to you. Whatever the addiction is, keep doing ho'oponopono. Be open to the next clue, opportunity, inspiration, or remedy. Then take inspired action and pursue it.

I love the old *Twilight Zone*. I grew up with it. I even got to meet Rod Serling, the creator of the series, in 1970, when I was in high school. It was a turning point because

I realized that if that little, scared, chain-smoking runt could become a famous author, then so could I. He was very human, and he was very nice to me. I had asked him if he would ever write an autobiography. The man was so humble, he said, "Nothing's really happened to me. It would be boring."

"Good lord," I thought. Man, he went through World War II. He was one of the early pioneers of civil rights movements and causes on television. One of the greatest scriptwriters of all time, and a great actor. He introduced all those *Twilight Zone* episodes, and later did the same in *Night Gallery*. He didn't think he had done anything worth reading about! Of course, after he died in 1975, other people wrote biographies of him, because his life *was* worth reading about.

One episode in particular struck me. It was written by Richard Matheson. God, it fried me. Here's this office worker. He's sitting at his desk, he's at the end of his day, and his secretary comes in. They're making plans for the next weekend. He's approving a flight or something like that. Then he gets up to do something, and then you hear this loud, booming voice yell, "Cut."

Everything freezes, including him. He's looking around, wondering, "What was that? Who yelled cut?" The walls of his office are being moved away. People come in and take his desk. Why? He's dazed and confused, and he's looking around. He realizes he's on a movie set, but this is his life. He didn't know he was on a movie set. He's at work. He is a supervisor, a manager or some sort, and he's running his business, but suddenly it's being disassembled, and he has to mentally process the idea that no, you're not at work; you're actually an actor in this studio. We just put you in the position of playing this role.

Please reflect on this, because it is a metaphor for life. You and I are both playing roles. What if God came in and took down all the walls around you? You'd think, "Wait a minute. I thought I was doing something important." The universe would say, "You were just playing a role. You don't need to do that anymore. We've got another role for you."

There are many implications that are worth meditating on here. For one thing, if you really look at life from the perspective of playing your role, you will be far less attached to it. You'll think, "Hey, this is my role right now. In a little bit, we'll finish the program." This detaches me from any worry, any concern, any heaviness in this moment.

This also ties to addictions, because if you're playing a role, part of your role right now is that of a person who has this particular addiction. If you're suddenly told, "You don't have that role. We changed the script. You had a habit, but we decided that's not really working, so we're going to change the script to where you have a positive addiction." There are negative addictions and positive addictions.

You're told, "You now have a positive addiction. From now on, this is your new role, is to say, *I love you, I'm sorry, please forgive me, thank you* several times a day. You don't have to say it all day long, just several times a day. You're almost addictive about it. It's almost as if you cannot do it. You have to get in your four phrases each day." Then you say to yourself, "This is my new script."

That *Twilight Zone* episode is a very hypnotic story. It's so inspired. I wish I had known Richard Matheson so I could have asked him, "How did you write that story? Where did it come from?" I know enough about him and other science fiction authors to know that these stories sometimes come to them from the whiteboard. They don't logically work out the idea; they receive it, flesh it out, and write it up. Then they give it to the producers, who say, "Yes, let's film that one." Then you and I, decades later, sit, marvel at it, thinking, "That was a work of genius." But they too were just doing their jobs. They were writing a script and producing a TV show that they hoped somebody would watch and sponsors would pay for.

From a ho'oponopono standpoint, the implications are deep. It brings us closer to God, to the whiteboard, to realize that we were given roles. As Shakespeare said, we're all actors, and we're on the stage of life. As generations pass, the stages and actors and costumes get changed. The show goes on.

You could even take a cleaning practice from that episode. If you understand that you are watching your behavior and are starting to go down an undesirable path, you can yell out yourself, "Cut." Interrupt your play. "I'm just playing this role. I don't have to go this way."

There's a series of psychological techniques called neurolinguistic programming, or NLP. One of these is the interrupt technique. They talk about finding ways to interrupt patterns of thought and behavior in yourself, or if you're a therapist, in a client. As you go through life and see yourself going where you don't want to go, you can yell, "Cut" in your head and pause. You say, "Wait a minute. I'm just playing a role. This is my set right now. This is my script. The script will change a little later. I'll get a new script."

If you really want to have fun, instead of waiting for the script to come in, rewrite it. "How would I like my character to be? I would like my character to be happy." All right. What does happy feel like? "I'd like my character to be less memory-driven and more inspiration-driven." All right, what does that look like?

You can have fun.

This is an advanced ho'oponopono technique right there. It's just pretend. You can even pretend you're Dr. Hew Len or Morrnah. If you were either one of those people, who have practiced ho'oponopono for decades and are considered its gurus, how would you act? How would you be? How would you think? What would you say? What would you feel? Even though you're not going to know any of this with 100 percent accuracy, you'll get closer to that feeling.

Another technique is what I've sometimes called the street sweeper of your life. The ancient Stoics would do a form of this practice. They would talk about imagining what the worst could be in order to prepare themselves for it. They weren't trying to create or attract it; they didn't know about the law of attraction two thousand years ago. They were trying to understand what could come up so they could mentally be ready for it, because they thought if they were mentally ready, they'd be able to handle virtually anything.

From the ho'oponopono standpoint, say you know something is coming up that could be unpleasant or negative: you're going to have a meeting, you're going to go to court, you're going to go see the doctor. You clean on your perception of that experience. Maybe you're thinking, "I'm going to go see my doctor, and they'll want to do a mammogram. I'm nervous about this." The nervousness is a memory; it's not inspiration. You're upset because memories of past experiences, past stories, and past beliefs are playing out right now. That's what you clean on and clear on. As you delete those feelings of insecurity and fear around doctors or surgery, as you focus on *I love you, I'm sorry, please forgive me, thank you* and *I forgives myself*, you delete those memories so that you can go and be in the moment. The Stoics armed themselves for war. With ho'oponopono, you're taking away the reasons for war to begin with.

Another method of cleaning is tapping. Originally its inventor, Roger Callahan, called it TFT, or Thought Field Therapy. Later it was called EFT, which is Emotional Freedom Techniques. From inspiration, I have added HFT: Ho'oponopono Freedom Technique. Guitar Monk Mathew Dixon and I have gotten together and created a whole certification program around HFT.

HFT blends tapping with ho'oponopono. Tapping is sometimes called *psychological acupuncture*. Thousands of years ago, in ancient China, they learned that there are energy meridians within the body. The fundamental principle of acupuncture is that your body is a meridian system with flowing energy channels. Think of them as rivers of energy going through you. When any of them has a block in it, the energy is not going all the way through. The acupuncturist puts a little needle where they perceive the block to be. Some people think they're blocking the energy, but they're unblocking it. They're actually creating an opening. It's as if there's a block in the river because there's garbage there. The acupuncturist sticks the needle in to remove the garbage. They're puncturing the block.

Roger Callahan discovered that rather than putting a needle in the point, you can tap on it to release stuck energy. We're tapping out the beliefs, the negativity, the limitation that we have found in our conscious awareness.

When I have a certain fear, it's considered to be a block in the body-mind system. Now that we know what it is, we tap on it, not to put it into our system, but to remove any and all blocks around it so that we're back to the natural flow of life. We're back to the natural flow of abundance. We're back to inspiration and choice.

This goes beyond healing a backache or headache. We're talking about the psychological issues that block us from having, doing, and being what we want, the things that keep us from attracting what we want or achieving our goals. You can tap those away.

I learned tapping decades ago because of my fear of public speaking. I've always been an introvert. I've always been a guy who'd be much happier just sitting in the library with a cup of coffee. But because I had to promote my early books and people would ask me to speak, I reluctantly went and spoke. I hated it and was terrified of it. I'd stand in front of a group of six people and nearly pass out because I couldn't breathe. I was hyperventilating. My brain was crushing my spirit.

I thought there had to be ways around this problem. Of course, there's Dale Carnegie; there's Toastmasters; there are all kinds of tools and books. Along the way, I discovered the five-minute phobia cure. Roger Callahan had an advertisement in an airline magazine for his five-minute phobia cure, which was a videocassette with a little book. It was about tapping away your fear of speaking. I got it and followed it.

Of course, now I speak. My largest live crowd was twenty thousand people, whom I addressed in Peru. My largest televised audience was probably in the millions, because I was on Larry King twice, Donny Deutsch's CNBC show, and many other shows.

I'd still rather be in the library drinking my coffee, but if I need to be in front of people, I can do it. Why? I tap away the fear.

The basic routine is tapping on the underside of your left hand, the carotid chop area, while making a statement: *Even though I feel*—and you fill in the blank—*even though I feel terrified of public speaking, I deeply love, accept, and forgive myself.*

Fill in the blank with the issue you want to remove: *Even though I am smoking too much, I deeply love, accept, and forgive myself. Even though I have to go to court, I deeply love, accept, and forgive myself. Even though my loved one left me, I deeply love, accept, and forgive myself. Even though sales are low, I deeply love, accept, and forgive myself.* This is the basic approach to tapping.

Then I go to the crown of my head, and I tap up there long enough and hard enough that it sounds as if I'm tapping on a door. I repeat the statement a couple times, then I go to the inside of the eyebrows above my nose and eyes, and I tap there while repeating the statement again.

I then go to the sides of the eyes near the temples, tap there, and repeat the statement. I go under the eyes, tap there, and repeat it. Then I go under the nose, where the little cleft is, down to the left collarbone. You tap these areas while making the same statement. Then I bring it down, and end with tapping the little fleshy part between the thumb and the first finger of the left hand. That's one round. Sometimes you only do one round on an issue, and you feel it's gone.

You could start by saying, *Even though I feel that I don't love myself, I deeply love, accept, and forgive myself. Even though I don't feel that I am worthy, I deeply love, accept, and forgive myself.* Even the phrase *I deeply love, accept, and forgive myself* sounds very much like ho'oponopono; it's very similar to the four key phrases. Just saying that is like doing ho'oponopono on your whole body.

We have blended tapping with ho'oponopono to create HFT. You can tap in any of the five basic phrases.

If you want to learn more about tapping, you can go on YouTube, where there are hundreds if not thousands of videos about it. One of my partners is Brad Yates, and we have a program called *Money beyond Belief.* He has hundreds of free videos. You can type in *tapping.* You can look up Brad Yates. You can type in *EFT* or *TFT,* and you will find a lot of basic ways of doing tapping. My friend Shalini has been teaching people how to tap away pain. You can type in the names of Shalini, Brad Yates, Roger Callahan, Guitar Monk, or me on your keyboard, and you'll learn all that you want to know about tapping.

Another advanced cleaning method is questioning beliefs. I call it the *option method*. Again, like with many of the advanced techniques, there's a whole world of information out there.

This method started when Barry Neil Kaufman had to do something for his autistic child. Everybody said, "We have no cures for autism. This is your throwaway child. Be glad you have a couple of other ones that are healthy."

Neither Barry nor his wife, Suzie, would accept that. They were inspired to mimic what their child did. If the child sat there and spun in circles, they sat there and spun in circles. If the child sat there and chattered something incomprehensible, they sat there and chattered too. Fundamentally, they were mirroring what the child was doing in order to signal, "We accept you just the way you are."

A lot of people think that you're just mirroring what the child is doing. That's not it, because underneath the mirroring is the idea, "We love you. We love you no matter what's going on. This is how you're communicating, so we're communicating in the same way back to you."

After Barry and his wife did that for years—it did take a long time—the autism left. Their son, Raun, got past it, and grew up to be an adult functioning in business, with no memory of autism.

Barry and Suzie went on to turn this into a dialogue system to work with fully functioning adults who had issues they wanted to work on. The Kaufmans found that the idea of total, nonjudgmental love and acceptance was therapeutic all by itself. That was what they were doing with their autistic son: "We love you just the way you are. We don't need to change anything. We're going to mirror what you are because we love you. We accept you."

This is very much like ho'oponopono: "We love you just the way you are." They Kaufmans were looking at their child probably as the Divine looks at us: "We love you. You think you're messed up or shortchanged or odd or different or eccentric, but we love you." This is why the fifth phrase, *I forgives myself*, is so powerful. The Divine forgives your little self for the "nasty little things" you've done. The Divine accepts you.

Just accepting somebody in the therapeutic process is powerful in its own right. Then Barry learned how to ask nonjudgmental questions like, "Why do you believe what you believe?" It's not threatening or judgmental, like, "Why in the world would you believe that?" It's not that kind of a question. It's more like, "Huh, that's curious. Why do you believe that?" Meaning, where did the belief come from? What's your evidence for the belief? This leads to other questions, like, do you believe your own evidence for the belief? It gets you to question your beliefs. As you question your beliefs and get to their root causes and origins, you dismantle them, you weaken them, and you can actually erase them.

When you look at your beliefs and realize, "That came from my father or my father or my aunt; it's not something I really want to believe," it goes; it's erased.

Other people have extended the work of Barry Neil Kaufman. My favorite has been Mandy Evans. Mandy has been my counselor, my therapist, my miracles coach, my healer since 1985. She's seen me go through the ups and downs of the extreme moments of life. I recommend Mandy Evans as another resource for option and questioning beliefs.

If you want to implement this method for yourself, ask yourself three basic questions: Do you believe that? Why do you believe that? What do you prefer to believe instead?

When you look at ho'oponopono and consider that it either comes directly from the Divine or from some source we can't even imagine, we start to realize that everything's made up. We don't understand how the world works. We don't know how it all began in any way that we can agree on. We don't understand our lives. Even when you look at psychology, there are different branches of psychology, and they don't all agree with each other. It's the same thing with science. Everybody worships science, but not all of the scientists agree. Some say, "God exists, and I've got proof." Others say, "There is no God, and I've got proof." Whom do you believe at this point?

For me, it's about bringing it down to the individual. I have to ask myself, what does it serve me to believe? Where did the belief come from? Do I still want to believe the evidence for that belief? What would it be better to believe?

We're looking for useful beliefs. For example, it is far more empowering to believe that God is on my side as I go through life, because the alternative sucks. I'm going to believe in faith. I'm going to believe I'm supported. I'm going to believe that inspiration will come to me as I keep doing ho'oponopono. I believe these things because I choose to, and they serve me.

That's the bottom line, when you ask that third question: what would I prefer to believe instead? If these beliefs aren't serving you, what would you prefer to believe? Then choose that.

I want to give a quick example. I've done a lot of work on helping people attract money. I've written books like *Attract Money Now* (it's free at Attractmoneynow.com), in which I say that our beliefs are keeping us from having more money.

For example, this is going to seem like a fact, but it's actually a belief: *the more money I spend, the less money I have*. Seems reasonable, right? If we actually live in a belief-driven, script-driven universe, like the *Twilight Zone* episode, so far the script has been written by the unconscious mind. But we want to consciously write the script, or let the Divine write the script from the whiteboard. Everything is up for grabs here, so why can't I change that belief too?

Decades ago, I kept telling myself, "The more money I spend, the more money I receive." It sounds counter-intuitive, illogical, even crazy: the more money I spend, the more money I receive. Well, guess what? That's my reality now.

I've told this story on stages. Once an accountant came up, and he said, "I'm an accountant, and I do taxes for people. You're absolutely right."

"I am?" I said.

"Yes. If you believe the money you spend is going to lead to more money that you will receive, you will unconsciously set that up to happen."

I have fun living life. I buy guitars and books, for other people as well as myself. When I'm writing the check, in my mind I think, "OK. I wonder where the replacement's coming from." I'm already thinking that more money's coming. Then by extension, I'll start thinking things like, "OK. I'm spending $5,000 right now. I'm expecting 50 grand. I don't know where, but I'm expecting 50 grand." Why? Because I chose a new belief.

This is very advanced ho'oponopono and probably very advanced in any level of creating your own reality or manifestation. You're creating your own reality by constantly deleting the things that aren't serving you, cleaning and clearing the limiting beliefs and choosing through inspiration the ones that excite you.

Someone in sales might decide they're not a good salesperson if they've had lots of rejections. But you can find any evidence for anything that you want to believe.

I've helped a lot of people come out with different books, including cookbooks. If you are into the paleo diet and you Google the evidence for it, you're going to get lots of it. Paleo wants you to eat like a caveman—lean meat and so forth. If you're into the vegetarian diet, which is the opposite of paleo, you're going to say, "Don't touch the meat." If you do a Google search for the evidence for a vegetarian diet, it will be overwhelming. If you want to find evidence for the low-carb diet, you'll easily find evidence for that. High carbs? I recently saw a diet that said, eat all the spaghetti you want; it's good for you.

You're sitting there with a buffet of evidence all around you. What do you choose? You have to choose what feels good to you, what matches your beliefs. You can find evidence for whatever you believe. I have evidence for my new belief that the more money I spend, the more money

I receive. An accountant walked up to me and said, "Hey, you're right."

There are hundreds, if not thousands, of practices out there if you research them. I do have favorites of my own. Ho'oponopono has the HA breathing technique: you breathe in slowly to the count of seven. With the out-breath, you can do HA HA HA, almost like laughing, to the count of seven. You breathe in to the count of seven, hold for seven, release for seven, hold for seven, and just keep that cycle going.

Many forms of meditation, including the HA meditation and Transcendental Meditation, give you something to focus on in order to occupy your mind. Years ago I saw a T-shirt that said, "Meditation is not what you think." I loved it because of the double meaning: If you think you know what meditation is, you don't. The second meaning is that whatever you're thinking is not meditation. As you're thinking, that's not actually meditation. Meditation is not what you think; meditation is behind what you think.

You can use the motto on that T-shirt as a kind of meditation. When you're sitting for fifteen or twenty minutes, thoughts are going on. Pay attention to the essence behind the thoughts: *I have thoughts. I'm not those thoughts.* See if you can see the whiteboard the thoughts are appearing on. See if you can feel the sky that the clouds—the thoughts—are appearing on.

Many meditations focus on breathing. Basically they direct you to get quiet, close your eyes, and pay attention to the air going into your nostrils. You follow it as it goes into your lungs. Then there's a pause before it comes back out. You can release the breath through your mouth or through your nose. Just being sensitive to that physiological experience brings people into the moment, so breathing meditation is powerful.

I even have a cigar meditation. I enjoy having cigars in the evening, and I often have them in the hot tub when I'm relaxing. My muscles are melting because of the heat of the hot tub, and the cigar is causing me to slow down my breathing. I look at the sky and say, "Thank you, thank you, thank you," as I look at all the stars. This is an extended ho'oponopono meditation. I certainly don't need a cigar to do it, but I call it a cigar meditation to suggest that you can make a meditation out of anything.

In Transcendental Meditation, which is one of the most popular and scientifically based meditation practices, they give you a mantra. When you sign up for your first course, they whisper your unique mantra into your ear. Whether it's actually unique to you or whether they whisper the same thing to everybody, I don't know. But they give you something to focus on in order to occupy the conscious mind.

I was with a spiritual teacher decades ago who said, "It doesn't matter if you repeat *Coca-Cola* in your head.

What matters is that the phrase is keeping you occupied so that you can allow the meditative process to take place behind it." At a certain point, your brain gets bored and fogged out by repeating *Coca-Cola*. At that point you can receive inspiration.

I have also found that reading books that totally absorb me is a meditation for me. I'm so totally occupied in the book that I'm oblivious to the rest of the world. I'm in a kind of trance. As I'm reading, something comes in. What was that something? Where did it come from? It was inspiration; we'll say it came from the whiteboard or from God or from the sky. What was occupying me was the meditation of reading. This may not be for everybody, but it works for me: reading a really engaging book does that.

There are many different ways to do meditation. I have never done yoga, but I know that it involves certain poses and postures. There's one in which you lie down as if you're dead in a coffin. You lie completely immobile on the floor, not moving anything, but with the awareness of everything around you. Your sensitivity is alive, but you don't move as if you're alive; you lie there as if you're dead. I have not done it, but I would imagine that it would be an incredibly sharp meditation experience to really get into the reality of "I'm not moving because I have died." What are you sensitive to? What are you feeling in that moment?

We don't want to overlook the idea that people could be inspired to do their own meditations. There could be different words or phrases that are unique to them, particularly if they're in another culture and know another language. There could be a word in that language that I don't know and which wouldn't mean anything to me, but it means something to them. Meditating on that, letting it roll around in the mind and soul, can bring them into that place.

I would again like to remind you about not paying attention to your thoughts. You have thoughts, but you're not your thoughts. Not paying attention to your emotions: you have emotions, but you're not your emotions. Not paying attention to your body: you have a body, but you're not your body. All of that is a meditation to lead you to the witness behind everything. Doing that is a meditative experience, which will lead people to the possibility of awakening.

In fact, the point of ho'oponopono is for you to become your own guru. It's taking your power back. Many of us look to the outside: "He knows better. She knows better. Dr. Hew Len knows better. Morrnah knows better." We dismiss our own inner knowingness and our own inner connection. The whole goal of this is, *you rely on you*. You become your own guru.

As Mandy Evans says, "Even when you go and solicit advice from other authors, speakers, counselors and therapists, how are you going to know what to believe?" She meant that ultimately you're going to trust yourself. Ultimately you're going to make a decision: "Oh, I like Dr. Hew Len, so I'm going to listen to what Dr. Hew Len has to say." We forget that we made that decision. We decided that we were smart enough to know that that person could be helpful to us. Then we unconsciously reverse it and put them on a pedestal, believing they know better but forgetting that actually we're the ones that put them on a pedestal. In fact, I must know better. I must know that that is useful for me.

Let's not forget that every book we come across, every audio we listen to, every seminar we go to, all the speakers, all the legends, all the orators, all the icons, all the thought leaders are only giving us their opinions.

8

Higher-Level Healing Philosophies of Dr. Hew Len

In this last chapter, I'd like to look a bit deeper into the man who communicated this philosophy to me: Dr. Hew Len. In particular, I'd like to discuss some of the other wisdom and philosophy that he has shared with me over the years. Let me discuss these concepts one by one and see what Dr. Hew Len meant by them. It's important to dig deeper into these philosophies since they contain more than it appears on the surface.

The first is, *you must accept total responsibility for yourself.* This means accepting total responsibility. Not just for what you think and do, but for what others think and do.

I still remember when I first talked to Dr. Hew Len over the phone and he told me about personal responsibility. I said, "Yeah, yeah, yeah, I know that. I've talked about personal responsibility."

But he said, "Have you ever heard the phrase, *you create your own reality*?"

"Yeah. I write about it. I teach it. I've tattooed it on people."

"Well, if you create your own reality and people show up that you don't like or that are triggering you in some way, you're creating them too."

I had to pause, because I had been saying you create your own reality, meaning that I'm responsible for what I personally say and do. But Dr. Hew Len was stretching it in a way I never considered. To judge from the responses I get from people, they've never considered this either.

This is why Dr. Hew Len stated that when he helped heal that entire ward of mentally ill criminals, it wasn't by only working on what he himself said and did: he had to accept responsibility for what those people had said and done. When he looked at their charts and saw that they were murderers and rapists who had committed very violent crimes and who were considered to be criminally insane, he had to look within himself and say, "I am responsible for them too."

This is a level of personal responsibility that I don't think any of us ever heard about when we were growing up. At most we were brought up hearing something to the effect of "You said it; you did it; you're responsible for it." A lot of people, especially ones stuck in victimhood, even shun that. They will excuse whatever they said and did by saying, "It's your fault. I did it because of you," or, "The devil made me do it," or, "Anybody but myself."

Empowerment is the stage where you do claim responsibility for what you're doing. That's where the phrase "If it's going to be, it's up to me" applies.

But in ho'oponopono, surrender is all about realizing that you're not here alone. Everything that anybody else does in your life experience—meaning that you are aware of it in some way, shape, or form—you helped create it in some way, shape, or form. This is total responsibility, and it is one of the biggest issues people have with ho'oponopono, because they don't want it. One person who attended an event said, "Total responsibility doesn't mean 100 percent responsibility; it means 200 percent responsibility, because you're responsible for everything you're doing and for everything everybody else is doing." Dr. Hew Len would say, "That's correct. You are 100 percent responsible for it all."

Although you are responsible, you aren't to blame. If I see or hear about some horrible event in the world, it almost may sound as if I'm to blame for that. But let me go back to what the Houston therapist said: "It is not your fault, but it is your responsibility." It is not your fault.

Yes, you are responsible for what your neighbor or boss or employee has done, but it's not your fault. You are not to be punished for it. You should not feel guilty about it or feel grief for it. Nonetheless, you are aware of it at this point, so you need to do something about it.

What are you going to do? You keep cleaning; you do the four phrases; you do the fifth phrase; you do whatever else you're inspired to do next. All of this is in the direction of solving or resolving a situation. It is not about standing still and flogging yourself because you think you did something wrong. You did nothing wrong. It is not your fault, but it is your responsibility to do something about it.

Jen Sincero is a friend of mine who has written bestselling books. The first one is called *You Are a Badass*, and I love it. She's a great lady, with a great sense of humor. This is what stood out in the book for me: "It's not your fault if you have been screwed up. After this point, it is your fault if you stay screwed up." She is playfully pointing out that up to now you were pretty much unaware; up to now maybe you never heard of the idea of 200 percent responsibility, but now you have. Now you have to do something about it, because you are responsible. Again, it's not your fault, but it is your responsibility.

Dr. Hew Len has also said that cleaning is his only purpose; he's only here to clean and clear. What is he cleaning and clearing on? Everything that shows up in his life experience. This means that when I showed up in his life experience, he had to clean on me. That time when I left him in a hotel room in Wimberley, Texas, and came back to find him watching the news, he was watching it to see what was triggering him. And what was triggering him was what needed to be cleaned and cleared.

Why is this important? Because we want to get to the fourth stage, the stage of awakening. At the fourth stage of awakening, as I understand it, there's nothing there to clean on. There's nothing there to trigger us. We have transcended it all. Dr. Hew Len's whole goal, his whole mission, is to clean and clear so he can be at the state of tranquility, the state of enlightenment, the state of awakening, the state of merging in consciousness at the fourth level.

Cleaning and clearing may be a full-time job that extends over lifetimes, depending on who's doing it and the grace of the gods. The goal is to get clear of everything that interferes in the miracle of now. That's how important it is. If Dr. Hew Len stops cleaning and clearing at any moment, he falls behind, in a sense. He falls behind in the path towards enlightenment.

It's the same thing for me. As I keep cleaning and clearing, *I love you, I'm sorry, please forgive me, thank you* is going on as a background loop in my head. All of this is to keep me in the moment and to keep me cleansing the moment so that I can get out of the way and allow inspiration. As long as I keep doing that, I'm moving closer to the grace of awakening. I believe that's what Dr. Hew Len was telling me. My only job is to clean.

Dr. Hew Len said that you can see only when you have the eyes of a newborn baby. For a newborn, life is a true miracle, a discovery, a dazzling world of color and sounds of unexpected joys. When we reach maturity, we've seen a lot, we've done a lot, we've been disappointed by a lot. We've got our filters, our belief systems, our limitations. We have ideas about what's possible; we're convinced that certain things are limitations and that there is no way to change them. Because we're adults and we know better, we have created the world of limitations on our eyesight.

Recently I had coffee with Lisa, my partner. A five-year-old child wandered over behind us, singing to herself. She was humming something I'd never heard before. Lisa and I started laughing in admiration of her youthful innocence. Neither of us would stand up and hum and sing as we went to get our coffee refilled, but the little one, still being so close to the newborn, with a face of purity, was still coming from "I feel like singing, so I'm going to sing. I feel like humming, so I'm going to hum. I'm over here playing with the coffee cups. I don't even know what coffee cups are. I don't even know what coffee is. I can't even taste coffee. I'm not allowed to have coffee, but isn't it cool? These cups are colorful, and they're pretty, and they have nice textures to them." That's the newborn's view of the world.

I don't have kids, but I've seen kids, puppies, and kittens when they're born. They're discovering life with an enthusiasm that I've lost. Rarely does it come back. But it can, and wow, it's available to me. I need to tap into it more.

Although the newborn has that innocence and purity, it's not exactly a blank slate, because as I mentioned earlier, we come in with some preprogramming. But for the most part there is an innocence there; we've just come from zero. We're closer to at-zero, to the experience of unlimited joy. In many ways, we just left God's lap. We still remember the warmth of that lap, so we're closer to joy and appreciation of being unlimited beings.

Dr. Hew Len has another maxim: *clean and let go; clear and trust.* In my book *The Secret Prayer,* I wrote, "There's really a three-step formula for making prayer work." It was heavily influenced by my work with Dr. Hew Len and my understanding of ho'oponopono.

As I've said, the very first step is to be grateful. The only thing that we should really be saying in prayer is thank you. If we truly look at our lives and realize all we've been given and all we're still being given, it's mind-boggling. It would crush our human ego to really accept the fact that we are given such life, such beauty, such bounty. The air, the planet, the things that keep us alive— we don't do anything about them, we just accept them and take them for granted. We rarely stop and say, "Thank you for that." That's beyond being grateful for your kids or your spouse, or where you live or the ability to do the work that you're doing. Same with me, with what I get to do. I'm living my life. I'm living my joy. I'm following my dream, living my passion, writing books, doing wonderful things like this book, which can make a difference for readers. That moves us into the first stage of gratitude, where prayer needs to begin: thank you. Mean it, really mean it; get it there in your soul.

The second step is making a request. Dr. Hew Len talked about prayer as a petition. Most of the time, we want something: I'm with a partner who is ill; I want her to feel better. I want this book to do fantastically in the world; I want it to make a difference in people's lives. I want them to wake up to a higher state of consciousness and become enlightened because of what I'm doing.

I would make those as petitions. My sister is not in good health, so I would make a petition that said, "Please heal Bonnie. I want her to be healthy and happy, wealthy and wise." All of that is in the area of the second step of the secret prayer.

The third step is letting go. Letting go goes back to faith, to trust, to the underlying fundamental principle in ho'oponopono, which says that the universe, God, Gaia is listening and acting and responding.

Years ago I taught a workshop called "The Manifestation Weekend." I talked about going to the whiteboard. I said, "When you're at the whiteboard, you can receive inspiration. But you can also deliver a request. That's where you want to tell the Great Something, 'This is what I would like to have do or be.'" This is where it could tie into the law of attraction, which is very much about the second phase: empowerment.

In this letting go phase, you tell the Great Something, "Here's my request," and you let go of it. You don't have a need for it. You don't have an addiction to it. You don't have an attachment to it. You definitely have a preference—otherwise you wouldn't have made the petition to begin with—but you're letting go and trusting that it will happen or not in its own good time. You're not in control; the Great Something is. In my book the *Attractor Factor*, which was a law of attraction bible for a lot of people, I say, "When you state your goal, which is similar to stating your intention, you end it with the phrase 'This, or something better.' Here's what I would like to have happen, but this or something better." The ancient Stoics had a reserve clause: "This is what's going to happen unless the gods, or faith"—they used the term *faith*—"want it otherwise." Prayer is a petition, but you've got to have faith, you've got to have gratitude, and you've got to let go.

Dr. Hew Len also teaches that clarity is the most important asset in your life. I remember being at a seminar with him. "How do you make a decision?" I asked. "How do you know which way to go? You've got plan A and plan B; how do you know which one to choose?"

He said, "When you are clear, there's no choice."

I repeated this to everybody in the room and they all said, "Ah!" They got it.

When you're clear, there's no choice, because you don't need to think about it. You are faced with a decision, but because of your clarity of consciousness, there is no moment when you are deliberating, "Should I go left or should I go right?" You know which way to go, because you're clear.

Ho'oponopono helps us to get clear. The more we do ho'oponopono, the more we do the clearing, the four phrases, the fifth phrase, or anything else that is in alignment with getting clear of our limiting beliefs, the more we move into the natural path and river of life. I don't have to think, because I'm clear. If I have to think, it could mean that I'm not clear yet. I still have to clean on the memories and the limitations so I'm in a place of inner knowing. My inner knowing tells me that this is what to do.

Why do I have this inner knowing, this clarity? It's because I've diluted the memories. They've been washed, they've been cleaned, they've been cleared, and I'm now at a place of pure clarity of consciousness.

Another maxim of Dr. Hew Len: *it's not the person; it's the program*. Once I was on a radio show with Dr. Hew

Len. They had people call in, and one guy called in. He was belligerent, mean, and negative. I was embarrassed. I was thinking, "Oh my God. My guru, my zero limits guy is here, and these people are calling in and tearing him a new one. What is going on?"

The station cut to a commercial break. I apologized to Dr. Hew Len. I said, "I had no idea what show we were going on. I didn't know that they would have call-ins; I didn't know that there'd be a caller like this."

Dr. Hew Len was as calm as he could be, and he said, "It's not the person; it's the program."

At first I thought that he meant the radio program, but he didn't: he meant the unconscious wiring of the person who was calling. And I realized this profound lesson: that person was calling because of a belief system. He had a view of the world, a mental paradigm. This man is as loving and as blessed by God as anybody else, but at some point he received programming that made him negative and angry. He received this mental program like a robot, which doesn't even know it's programmed; it's just living out the program. He gets triggered because of his programming, so he calls and tears Dr. Hew Len up. He isn't doing it because he is inherently evil; he's doing it because of his program. When I realized that, tears came to my eyes. Every single person has been programmed, all of us: you, me, everybody.

When I was homeless in Dallas in the seventies, I had a different program than I do today. I looked out at the world and saw it as being against me. I was totally alone, sad, depressed. I certainly wanted to make a difference with my writing, but it was very much a solo experience. I looked at the world, and I saw lack, limitation, scarcity, negativity, evil, and threats everywhere.

I don't feel that way today. Physically, I'm the same guy (although I'm quite a bit older), but the program I have now is different from the program that Joe had back in the 1970s.

You know what's different? I was able to erase and delete the old program, install a lot of new programs, and get to the point where I'm more in the natural flow of life.

The bottom line for me is a reminder that if you deal with people who seem to be threatening or negative or hurtful, you've got to remember that it's not that person, it's their program.

When you clean on yourself, when you clear using *I love you, I'm sorry, please forgive me, thank you, I forgives myself,* or other cleaning tools, you help delete that program.

The rule of thumb is, if you can see a program in somebody else, you've probably got it in you too. As Jung said, if you're upset about the behavior of somebody else, you probably have that same quality in you. From the ho'oponopono standpoint, you don't try to change the other person. You try to delete the program in you. As you delete it in you, the other person's got to change or move away, or you will no longer be upset about them, because that program will have been disconnected.

The next maxim is: *you are already perfect.* When people first hear that, they may think, "Well, I can already be perfect, but I need to clean, because I have imperfections."

Think back to what I said at the beginning of this book: the key division is our separation as individuals from Divinity. We begin with that separation and then we break it up further, because we feel alone.

Dr. Hew Len is saying that you are already divine. Your inner essence is that purity from the whiteboard. Behind the persona, behind the beliefs, behind the program, behind the separation, behind the illusion, you are absolutely perfect. This is looking to the core you. This is looking beyond your memories, your belief systems, your self-image—any of the ways you might consciously or unconsciously describe yourself. We're looking to Source; in you is Source.

It's like taking a drop of water and saying, "You're the ocean." The drop is going to say, "I'm not the ocean at all; I'm a little drop of water." No, you are the ocean, you're from the ocean, you are reflecting the ocean, you are, in essence, the ocean. You are divine. You are God. You are a part of the whiteboard. You are inspiration itself. The Buddhists speak of the original face. The original face of you is perfect.

Another maxim: *data speaks, and you speak data, so you are not in control anywhere.* That sounds confusing at first. But for Dr. Hew Len, data is all of the belief chatter, all of the mind stuff that separates us from Divinity. It's very easy for us to get caught up in it. Even as you're reading this book, you're filtering it through your own data. You're reading this information, but you're seeing it as data going in and matching and meeting your own data. Where it matches your data, you'll say, "Oh, that Dr. Joe is a cool guy. He says stuff I believe in." Where the data doesn't match, because you have a different filtering system, you'll say, "Man, he was off in a lot of places. I don't agree with everything he had to say." Or maybe it'll be dismissal: "Forget him. He's off on another planet someplace."

In many ways this data is keeping us from the enlightenment that's behind all the data. Behind it all is actually the whiteboard, that purity, pure zero consciousness, where everything begins and everything is alive. We're writing on the whiteboard: we're writing data, we're writing our belief systems. Psychology says that everyone has a different reality because of their belief systems, which are based on their upbringing and background. If I point to a glass of water and say, "Here's a glass of water," you will agree that it's a glass of water, but internally you see a different glass than I do. We're using data terms to get close to agreeing on what reality is.

As long as we talk about something neutral, like a glass of water, there's no argument. But what if we start talking about something more sensitive? I may say, "This person over here is a good person." You're looking at the same person, but you see a different reality because of your belief system.

Your belief systems are the data that Dr. Hew Len is referring to. At seminars, he sometimes got a little impatient with people, who would keep asking questions, and he would say, "All the questions are bullshit." When somebody asked a question, you could see that it was coming from the mind, which is full of data. What is behind the mind? What is behind the data? What is behind the personality? Where is the perfection? That's where ho'oponopono and Dr. Hew Len are pointing. When you really take it on, you say, "Man, if I ask one more question, I'm just proving that I'm not enlightened. I've got to shut up and realize that even the urge to ask questions is an urge from the data to extend the data. We want to transcend that and go to what's behind it."

The last point I want to highlight is, *you don't need intentions; allow the Divine to inspire you.*

When I was in the movie *The Secret*, I got a copy of the DVD and gave it to Dr. Hew Len. He held it, turned it over, looked at me, and said, "I'll put it on a shelf."

"Wait a minute. You're not even going to watch it?"

He does things like that, because he will get a sense of a thing, he'll be tuned into what it is, and because he's clear, he knows if it's useful to him or not at that point. Maybe later he watched it; who knows?

For Dr. Hew Len, the law of attraction and stating intentions were really ways to extend data and live from more limitations. When I first heard this, I was a little offended, but I was open-minded enough to hear him out. For him, stating an intention is stating something you'd like to have do or be based on what your data believes is possible. It's based on what you've already read, what you've already done, what you've already heard, what you believe can be in the realm of possibility. But that's all tightly confined within a belief system that allows you to think that way.

What Dr. Hew Len wants to do is delete the data system. The data system is the limitation. Even if you believe anything is possible, that's a new data system. Even the phrase *anything is possible* is out of a new data system. It's a better and more empowered data system than victimhood, but it's still a built-in system of limitations.

Dr. Hew Len always focused on listening to the Divine. When the Divine gives inspiration, act on it.

I've already said that I think intentions are for wimps; I prefer inspirations. The way I like to word it is, my inspirations are my new intentions. When I receive an inspiration to create something, I just look at it as my next assignment. The inspiration is now the intention. I'm letting it come from the whiteboard, from the Divine, rather than from the restricted ego consciousness, which would say, "This is possible, and this would be cool." The inspiration could blow my mind, because it comes from something wider and deeper than my own mind.

In conclusion, I want to say I'm grateful. All of us should practice gratitude as a takeaway from this book. The heart of ho'oponopono is realizing that you're already living the miracle; you're already perfect. The only thing between you and the miracle of now is the data. And that data, which consists of beliefs, a mindset, and the stories that we bought into, can be cleaned and cleared. Whether it's *I love you, I'm sorry, please forgive me, thank you* or the new fifth phrase, *I forgives myself,* or whatever it takes, use it as the device to take you to the next level.

As a reader of this book, you're probably not into victimhood. You've already moved past it to the level of empowerment. But there's surrender, which is where ho'oponopono lives, and there's also awakening. We want to work on ourselves. Our only job, really, is to work on ourselves, because, as ho'oponopono teaches, there is nobody else out there. It's me; it's you. Whatever modality you use, keep doing it, because it's freeing you.

As Dr. Hew Len says, as you free yourself, you free the world. As you clean a limitation from your own consciousness, you remove it from the collective consciousness of the world. This is huge. It means that working on yourself is saving the planet. Working on yourself is a noble cause that expands and enriches every single person.

Whatever method you use, don't stop. Get up every morning, practice, make time for meditation, and do ho'oponopono whenever it feels right for you. Tune into the silence, because actually the silence isn't quiet. And finally, expect miracles.

Index

About the Author

D r. Joe Vitale is a globally famous author, marketing guru, movie, TV, and radio personality, musician, and one of the top 50 inspirational speakers in the world.

His many bestselling books include *The Attractor Factor*, *Attract Money Now*, *Zero Limits*, *The Miracle: Six Steps to Enlightenment*, and *Anything Is Possible*.

He's also recorded numerous bestselling audio programs, from The Missing Secret and The Zero Point to The Power of Outrageousness Marketing and The Awakening Course.

A popular, leading expert on the law of attraction in many hit movies, including The Secret, Dr. Vitale discovered the "missing secret" not revealed in the movie. He's been on Larry King Live, Donny Deutsch's "The Big Idea," CNN, CNBC, CBS, ABC, Fox News: Fox & Friends and

Extra TV. He's also been featured in *The New York Times* and *Newsweek*.

One of his most recent accomplishments includes being the world's first self-help singer-songwriter as seen in 2012's *Rolling Stone Magazine*. To date, he has released seventeen albums! Several of his songs were recognized and nominated for the Posi Award, regarded as "The Grammys of Positive Music."

Well-known not only as a thinker, but as a healer, clearing people's subconscious minds of limiting beliefs, Dr. Joe Vitale is also an authentic practitioner of modern Ho'oponopono, certified Reiki healer, certified Chi Kung practitioner, certified Clinical Hypnotherapist, certified NLP practitioner, Ordained Minister, and Doctor of Metaphysical Science.

He is a seeker and a learner; once homeless, he has spent the last four decades learning how to master the powers that channel the pure creative energy of life without resistance, and created the Miracles Coaching® and Zero Limits Mastery® programs to help people achieve their life's purpose. He lives in the Austin, Texas area.

His main site is www.MrFire.com.